The Crosby Arboretum

Reading the American Landscape

LAKE DOUGLAS, SERIES EDITOR

The Crosby Arboretum

A SUSTAINABLE REGIONAL LANDSCAPE

Robert F. Brzuszek   ❊   *Foreword by* Neil G. Odenwald

LOUISIANA STATE UNIVERSITY PRESS

BATON ROUGE

Publication of this book is made possible in part by the generous support of Lynn and Stewart Gammill, Deborah and Osmond Crosby, and Crosby Land & Resources.

Published by Louisiana State University Press
Copyright © 2014 by Robert F. Brzuszek
All rights reserved
Manufactured in China
First printing

Designer: Laura Roubique Gleason
Typefaces: Minion Pro text with MrsEaves display
Printer and binder: Everbest Printing Co. through Four Colour Imports, Ltd., Louisville, Kentucky

Frontispiece: Pinecote Pavilion. Photo courtesy Megan Bean/Mississippi State University.

Front cover images: Photos of Pinecote Pavilion, the Slough weir, and the Savanna Exhibit are by Ed Blake Jr., courtesy of Marilyn Blake. Photo of the Forested Stream Exhibit is by the author.

Back cover image: Photo of Pinecote Pavilion and Piney Woods Lake is by Lynn Gammill, courtesy Crosby Arboretum.

LIBRARY OF CONGRESS CATALOGING-IN-PUBLICATION DATA

Brzuszek, Robert F., 1959–
 The Crosby Arboretum : a sustainable regional landscape / Robert F. Brzuszek ; foreword by Neil G. Odenwald.
  p. cm. — (Reading the American landscape)
 Includes bibliographical references and index.
  ISBN 978-0-8071-5433-5 (cloth : alk. paper) — ISBN 978-0-8071-5434-2 (pdf) — ISBN 978-0-8071-5435-9 (epub) — ISBN 978-0-8071-5436-6 (mobi) 1. Crosby Arboretum (Picayune, Miss.) 2. Arboretums—Mississippi—Picayune. 3. Landscape architecture—Mississippi—Picayune. I. Odenwald, Neil G. II. Title. III. Series: Reading the American landscape.
 QK480.U52M73 2014
 712.09762′15—dc23

2013021579

The paper in this book meets the guidelines for permanence and durability of the Committee on Production Guidelines for Book Longevity of the Council on Library Resources. ♾

This book is dedicated to
the life and creative spirit of
Edward L. Blake Jr. (1947–2010).

Robinson Photography

As mind and spirit seek expression, the landscape is the medium
through which we re-shape our shelter, the Earth.

—EDWARD L. BLAKE JR.

The Savanna Exhibit

Photo by Ed Blake Jr., courtesy of Marilyn Blake

CONTENTS

Herbaceous understory, Dead Tiger Natural Area

ILLUSTRATIONS

FOREWORD

Emotions ran high when I was invited to write the foreword to *The Crosby Arboretum,* by Robert Brzuszek, a former graduate student of memorable abilities and sensitivities. In addition to having warm feelings for Bob and regard for his work in graduate studies at Louisiana State University, I have other personal ties to this special site. Edward L. Blake Jr., a central figure in the ongoing development of the arboretum, was a student in my first class as a teaching assistant at Mississippi State University in the late 1960s. Further, in the early days following the founding of the arboretum, I served on its board of directors. Consequently, as I read through the manuscript for the first time, I experienced an emotional journey; a host of personal feelings for the people associated with the arboretum and the site itself rose to new heights.

Bob has done a masterful job of telling the comprehensive story of the Crosby Arboretum, from the initial visionary concept of the Crosby family for a memorable garden setting to commemorate the life of their own L. O. Crosby Jr. to the arboretum's esteemed position among unique arboreta in the United States today. Numerous aspects of this engaging story are noteworthy.

First, any reference to the Crosby Arboretum must address the many contributions made by Blake, the key figure in the arboretum's early development. The untimely passing of this giant of a man—in both physical stature and design theory and practice—left many of us wondering how Blake's wisdom in words and sketches could be not only preserved but shared with everyone who aspires to think conceptually about problem solving in the natural environment. Brzuszek's day-to-day work experience over many years with Blake and his comprehensive examination of Blake's personal papers give us powerful first-hand insights into how seriously Blake took that problem solving. During those early days on the board, we would inquire at meeting after meeting when we could expect the final draft of the Master Plan for the arboretum. Ed would invariably ask for patience and understanding as he struggled through the minute details of the evolving plan that ultimately took nearly ten years to complete. What a revolutionary plan it turned out to be! Few can comprehend the value of the in-depth study Ed gave to what for many of us was a lackluster, forsaken Piney Woods site in south Mississippi. Only Ed Blake could bring such magic and enlightenment to the treasures hidden in the Crosby Arboretum site. In his words, he "listened and found his voice" at the Crosby Arboretum.

The highly acclaimed Crosby Arboretum is an example of a project where the design process guided a large number of specialists through many hours of study and experimentation. Defining a clear mission at the beginning set the parameters, and all embraced that vision from the initial site analysis to continuing evaluation, which is ongoing to this day. There is a wholesome balance between the biological requirements associated with the Crosby landscape and the aesthetic principles that everyone aspired to have for this award-winning project.

"Journey," "sense of discovery," "anticipation," "evolving," "ecology of place" are but a few of the descriptive, compelling words and phrases that make us want to experience this special place, either for the first time or on repeat visits, because every visit is a new experience at the Crosby Arboretum. While the home site is a dynamic and ever-changing microcosm that focuses on the indigenous plants of the Pearl River Drainage Basin, there is so much more in the associated natural areas within an hour's drive of Picayune. These sites help to tell the fuller, more comprehensive mission and story of the Crosby Arboretum.

Because design is a central, guiding theme in the unfolding story of the Crosby Arboretum, this book should be required reading for all aspiring designers, including architects and landscape architects. It speaks clearly about how there can be a beautiful integration between site structures and the landscape, establishing a true "sense of place."

On a personal note: Bob Brzuszek is uniquely qualified to write a book on the Crosby Arboretum. He is most unselfish and quite modest in his telling of the story and his personal contributions to the arboretum. Bob spent thirteen of his most creative years exploring every parcel of the Crosby landscape. He immersed himself in the mission, the Master Plan, the hopes and dreams of Ed Blake and the board of directors, and executed through experimentation and required modifications, through "landscape editing," much of what we enjoy at the arboretum today. Fortunately, Bob continues to guide this development in addition to his teaching and research responsibilities at Mississippi State University.

Neil G. Odenwald, FASLA
Professor Emeritus
Louisiana State University

PREFACE

The Crosby Arboretum is a garden for the next century.

—J. C. Raulston, horticulturist, quoted in *Garden Design*
magazine, 1996

This is a story about place. It originates in a most unlikely location—
in the scrubby pine fields of south Mississippi. The Interpretive Center of the Crosby
Arboretum, Mississippi State University Extension, lies on the fringe of a railroad
town known as Picayune, Mississippi. Nearly equidistant between the bustling cities
of New Orleans, Louisiana, and Gulfport, Mississippi, Picayune was once described
by literary critic Noel Polk as an area that falls between real places.[1] But those who live
in Mississippi or in other rural areas know these nether regions contain cultural and
biological treasures. While they may be short on museums and coffee shops, they are
rich in pine forests, grasslands, and biodiversity. They do not offer glass-towered office
buildings, but they instead fuel our imaginations. These seemingly desolate regions of
backwater swamps and wetlands, pastures and farms, are dotted with faded hamlets
and roadside churches. They have been largely spared from thoughtless development
schemes because of the lack of capital investment. It may be this "nothingness" that
gives pause for people here to dream inspired dreams without much influence from
the outside world.

I was a young graduate student in landscape architecture when I first heard of
the Crosby Arboretum. The year was 1987, and Pinecote Pavilion had just been constructed. I attended a lecture given by the Crosby Arboretum's first director, Edward L. Blake Jr., who spoke on the topic of wildflowers. But he spoke little of wildflowers, shifting the topic instead to the broader realm of Gulf Coast ecosystems and
even the universe's whirling galaxies. I knew there was something special going on at

this newly formed public garden, but I couldn't quite place what it was. I needed to find out more.

The next summer Blake invited me to assist him in mapping the savanna exhibits, and later to assist on biological surveys at the Crosby Arboretum's natural areas. My curiosity about how the Crosby Arboretum was designing its landscape exhibits led me to explore this topic in my graduate thesis. Under the heading "Establishing Spatial Patterns for the Beech-Magnolia Exhibit in the Crosby Arboretum of Picayune, Mississippi," I applied what I was learning at Crosby to craft the design ideas for one of the arboretum's plant community exhibits.[2] Although I wasn't versed in beech woodlands or ecology, I went to the forest to learn. I walked through older woodlands and along stream banks and recorded what I observed. I looked for visual cues that would reveal their hidden secrets. It took about a year of wandering in the woods before the vegetation patterns that I saw revealed their inner workings. I understood the ecological relationships and appreciated the landscape forms they took. Ultimately, this is what the design of the landscape exhibits at the Crosby Arboretum was truly about—celebrating the processes and patterns of nature in our own regional settings.

After I finished my graduate studies, Ed Blake gave me a call to meet him at the Crosby Arboretum. The facility was going to open full-time to the public, and he was in need of a person to help him complete the Master Plan and develop the exhibits, to build the educational programs, and to develop the site infrastructure. He asked me if I was that person. I said yes, and I served first as curator and then as site director for the next thirteen years. It took a while for me to recognize it, but eventually I realized that my role at Crosby was to serve as a translator. At first this was accomplished by communicating Crosby's mission to the arboretum's visitors; then in its site development, programming, interpretive signage, and brochures; and later in the introduction of new interpretive technologies and teaching. I viewed the implementation of the Crosby Arboretum's goals as a grand experiment that had no certain outcome. There were many unanswered questions and challenges to make it work as it was originally envisioned. There are still challenges today.

This is the story of how the Crosby Arboretum came to be. I have provided as many references to original sources as possible and have included much from my personal experiences and knowledge. There are many, many people to thank for their contributions, interviews, insights, and reviews for this book. I greatly appreciate Lake Douglas for his inspiration, suggestions, and enthusiasm throughout the book's progress. Bill Thames and Renee Clary had remarkable patience and helpful comments in the early editing. Crosby Arboretum founders Lynn Crosby Gammill and Osmond Crosby III, and the arboretum's first registrar, Katherine Furr, generously reviewed the chapters on the arboretum's beginnings. Leslie Sauer, Carol Franklin and Colin Franklin of Andropogon Associates, and Robert Poore of Native Habitats provided important feedback on the early design steps. Crosby Arboretum Foundation board members Ruth Cook and Fay Bright offered helpful comments on recent arboretum history. I owe special thanks to Christopher Wells, former Crosby Arboretum botanist, and to Crosby's first botanist, Dr. Sidney McDaniel, for their comments. The chapter on architecture was reviewed by Robert Ivy, executive director of the American Institute of Architects, and author of the book *Fay Jones*. Maurice Jennings, partner of Fay Jones, contributed his thoughts on architecture and his experiences during the design and construction of Pinecote Pavilion. I am grateful, too, for the review by Dr. Bill Wolverton, of Wolverton Environmental Services, on the Crosby Arboretum biological filter system. Professors Iain Robertson (University of Washington), Bob Grese (University of Michigan), and Dan Earle (emeritus, Louisiana State University) added valuable dialogue on the role of this ecological garden.

Deep affection goes out to Crosby Arboretum board members Dorothy Crosby, Mary Hough, Cameron Man, Julia Anderson, Anne Bradburn, Doug Wilds, Jane McKinnon, Yvette Rosen, Sadik Artunc, and Dr. Neil Odenwald. Thanks to the Crosby Arboretum, Mississippi State University Extension Service staff, who work great wonders with little resources: Pat Drackett, director; Richelle Stafne, senior curator; burn manager and maintenance supervisor extraordinaire Terry Johnson; multitalented Kim Johnson; amazing artist Robin Whitfield; and maintenance assistant and all-around great guy, Jarrett Hurlston. And to those in the Mississippi State University administration who believe in the Crosby Arboretum: Dr. David Veal, Dr. Patricia Knight, Dr. Vance Watson, Dr. George Hopper, Dr. Greg Bohach, and Dr. Gary Jackson. To the past employees of the Crosby Arboretum, who have labored long and hard to make it succeed: Caroline McGavock, Karen Hull, Tammy Schock, Nelda Lee, Sue Bond, Sidney Noel-Clukey, Joe Gomez, Becky Hennop, Dr. Chen-Zi Tang, Janine Conklin, Georgia Bilberry, and Melinda Lyman. To the Crosby Arboretum volunteers and members, past and present, with fondness to Sallye Hammett, Will Sullivan, Anne Breaux, Fran Meredith, Trish Blossman, Charlie and Julie Hunger, Allen and Julia Anderson, Jean and Paul McGinnis, Les Cambias, Trish Blossman, Oscar Eckhoff, Allen Lowrie, Dixie McDonald, Dot Burge, Marc Pastorek, Jane Flower, Jean Hartfield, Alice Holmes, Garrett Newton, Nell Kieff, George and Ginnie Barry, and so many others. Thanks to Paddi, John, and Nicole for being there. A heartfelt thanks to those leaders in the native plant movement in the Deep South who were so important in the arboretum's early days, and who are my true heroes: Tommy and Thayer Dodd, Darrell Morrison, Plato Touliatos, Bill Fontenot, Margie Jenkins, Johnny Mayronne, Larry Lowman, Charles Allen, Rick Webb, Gail Barton, Halla Jo Ellis, and Peter Loos. To the folks that have inspired me deeply to *think:* Felder Rushing, Dan Overly, Frank Chaffin, Chuck Fryling, Suzanne Turner, Wayne Womack, and Jon Emerson. To the next generation of environmental researchers (students and faculty) that will carry the work at Crosby forward with very capable hands—most notably Dr. Tim Schauwecker. And to the many Crosby Arboretum friends over the years, too many to mention here but you know who you are.

Special thanks to Marilyn Blake, Ed's wife and partner for many years, who allowed me to pore over his private journals. One observation that strikes me now, thirty years after the beginning of the Crosby Arboretum, is that the novel advances made in the arboretum's fledgling days are still relatively new concepts today. Only now are we recognizing the value and importance of nurturing nature in all environments, including the most urban of our communities, and we have so much more to learn. May we continue to design and create places that not only regenerate life but inspire the human heart.

The Crosby Arboretum

THE LAND AND ITS PEOPLE

Much of it is covered exclusively with the long leaf pine; not broken, but rolling like the waves in the middle of the great ocean. The grass grows three feet high and hill and valley are studded all over with flowers of every hue. The flora of this section of the State and thence down to the sea board is rich beyond description. Our hortus-siccus, made up on this hurried journey, would feast a botanist for a month.

—John F. H. Claiborne, *A Trip through the Piney Woods,* 1840

Like the deep sedimentary soils that it rests upon, south Mississippi is composed of many layers. The coastal cities of Biloxi and Gulfport contour their shorelines along the Gulf of Mexico with brightly lit casinos and miles of imported sandy beach. These waterside cities enjoy a steady industry of fishing, tourism, and ship building. But drive just a few miles north from these resort destinations and you will soon find yourself in the thick of the Piney Woods landscape. Lumberton, Kiln, and Fruitland Park are just a few of the small towns you encounter embellished with names that reveal their agricultural or timber origins. The people here are intimately tied to the soil with still-popular pastimes of hunting and fishing along the ample river systems. It is a sylvan land.

Connecting these small community centers are miles of two-lane asphalt roads that wind along abundant cattle pastures, forests, and scattered homesteads. Slender pine trunks line the roadsides and create alternating rhythms of sun and shadow in late afternoons that can dangerously lull a driver to sleep. Mississippi is often misunderstood nationally, and it is far too simple to believe you could sum up this region through the windshield. You must dig deep and fully engage the senses to understand what this land has to offer.

As you step out from the car, you are immediately confronted with the vagaries of this place, and there is no mistake that you have landed squarely in Mississippi. If it is midsummer, your clothes will abruptly wither in the moist subtropical heat and humidity. The air is almost thick enough to see and taste. Everything that surrounds you seems to be a little more magnified and larger than life. The leaves of southern magnolia (*Magnolia grandiflora*) and bigleaf magnolia trees (*Magnolia macrophylla*) are not just large here, but enormous. Cicadas do not merely buzz loudly in the trees but pierce the air with their droning sound. The unmitigated summer sun creates such an intense light that both animals and humans must retire midday into their warrens.

Mississippi's landscape has inspired noted fiction writers such as Eudora Welty, William Faulkner, and John Grisham. In a land so richly textured, authors merely have to reach out and pick their muse. If one looks closely, the stories are written into the land. Narratives are abundantly embedded in the interstices of the soil, water, and air and help give form to place. It is not uncommon to see slivers of the past all around—in the ruts of previously well traveled roadways now grown to forest; the brick steps that remain long after the house is gone; a rambling rose that was once planted by a forgotten hand. The southern landscape teems with the specters of those who have walked here before.

The Crosby Arboretum is a place where people can see and experience representations of the native environments of the Gulf Coastal landscape. The arboretum appears to be a remnant natural area, with woodlands, wetlands, and grasslands untouched by people. Yet, while inspired by nature, it was carefully shaped and thoughtfully guided by human interventions. It features natural-appearing places, yet little is natural. It is not a virgin landscape as in a preserve, but instead one that has healed from the effects of intensive farming and forestry. The Crosby Arboretum presents a rich case study of a human dialogue with the land. Rather than embracing prior worldviews that humans are somehow separate from the natural world, it is instead a bold conviction that humans interact with and are a partner of nature. At Crosby, the existing landscape was studied and understood and natural process was embraced. Historically, many botanic gardens and arboreta feature landscape exhibits that are formally structured and maintained to the smallest detail. The Crosby Arboretum is ordered in its layout yet allows for ecological process to occur.

The Crosby Arboretum is a place born from the land and its people. Unlike many notable architectural and landscape edifices, the Crosby Arboretum did not spring from the grand vision of just one person. Its design derived instead from a synergistic blend of the leading minds in the arts and sciences. Biologists, geologists, landscape architects, architects, horticulturists, artists, and foresters—all had gathered around this site to dream of its potential and to envision the type of landscape it could become. When the design for Crosby Arboretum's Master Plan was presented an Honor Award in 1991 by the American Society of Landscape Architects, the arboretum was described by the jury as the "first fully realized ecological garden in the country."[1] But in order to appreciate this unique garden that was built from the land, we first need to understand how the land was shaped and who lived there.

THE DISTANT PAST

The place that would one day become the Gulf Coast landscape once lay sleeping under a shallow blue sea. Spiraled ammonites and fierce aquatic reptiles such as mosasaurs swam freely above the ocean floors that over 70 million years later became the busy cities of Pensacola, New Orleans, and Houston.[2] Countless sunsets saw the nearby Appalachian and Ozark mountain ranges slowly wear down to the rounded mounds they resemble today. From these tall peaks, massive amounts of erosion occurred, so much so that the entirety of today's lower Coastal Plain was built upon thousands of feet of sediments, and the land emerged from the sea. It has been estimated that over the past 60 million years over 20,000 feet of sediments has been deposited in the central Gulf region.[3] As climates changed and glaciers inched their way across northern lands, rich soils and gravels coursed southward through ancient streambeds. Incessant winds blew a fine powdery dust from these faraway glacial moraines to lightly touch down along the Mississippi River corridor. During the Pleistocene Epoch, over two and a half million years ago, the Gulf Coastal Plain was mostly formed. Sand and silt grains steadily built the plain into a flat sedimentary landscape of mud. In many ways, the coastal landscape still bears a striking resemblance to the sea bottom that it once was—mostly flat with little elevation change, deep layers of sand and silt, and an infusion of water and waterways.

While the Gulf Coast can be defined in many ways, it has one unfailing characteristic that has recurred through the ages—an endless propensity for change. Here the rivers shift across the landscape like untamed beasts and repeatedly seek new courses. As they race along, they carve sediments from peaks and valleys, only to deposit them elsewhere. Even the large body of water known as the Gulf of Mexico couldn't quite make up its mind as its shoreline edge continuously shifted in a slow yet persistent fashion. Over eons, as the Earth's climate warmed and cooled, the vast northern ice sheets would wax and wane in size, causing the retreat or advancement of the world's oceans.[4] Like the shapeshifter that it is, the Gulf Coast region has changed continuously over geologic time. This region has one of the most resilient ecosystems on the North American continent because of its remarkable ability to rebound with new life.

Many natural forces keep the Gulf Coast landscape in a constant state of flux. The Gulf of Mexico interacts with its adjacent plain, contributing not only sea breezes and high humidity but also heavy rains, often in excess of sixty inches per year. Much of the immediate coastal area is wetland, and the vegetation is adapted to periods of nearly continuously wet soils. With unsettling regularity, fierce tropical storms and their accompanying tornadoes and lightning dance across the land. Studies of historic hurricane paths show most of the Gulf Coast landscape hit with alarming regularity. One study of historic weather patterns in Alabama concluded that hurricanes have visited the same areas on average every 318 years.[5] Massive hurricanes, monstrous storms, record floods, debilitating droughts, and devastating fires ravage the land here on so frequent a basis that old-growth forests hardly exist. Only in the most protected of deep coves and river basins of the Southeast are older woodlands typically found. This continual churning of fires and flood, tornadoes and hurricanes, droughts and devastation, gave rise to one of the most beautiful yet resilient landscapes in North America today—the Gulf Coast Piney Woods.

When Europeans arrived to colonize the North American continent over half a millennium ago, a vast pine savanna (a flat, open grassland with scattered trees) stretched inland along the Atlantic and Gulf coasts.[6] A nearly continuous band of pine had formed from the sand ridges of eastern Texas to the flat terraces of Virginia, broken apart only by the river valleys and wetlands, where hardwood trees abound.[7] This was the landscape of the majestic longleaf pine forest (*Pinus palustris*). Written accounts from the 1860s describe Mississippi as a landscape of pines and other trees with a shimmering understory of grasses and wildflowers.[8] Longleaf pines bend and sway in strong winds and can live the longest of all the pines.[9] If a pine can stand up to the fiercest storms, it may survive for hundreds of years. Mississippi's champion longleaf pine resides today in Jasper County and reaches 115 feet in height and nearly ten feet in circumference. This monster of a tree is estimated to exceed four hundred years in age.[10] Southern writer Janisse Ray, after visiting an ancient longleaf pine grove in Georgia, summed up the scene aptly: "Nothing is more beautiful, nothing more mysterious, nothing more breathtaking, nothing more surreal."[11] Just a few hundred years ago, the original longleaf pine range encompassed over ninety million acres. Today, with less than 3 percent of its original holdings left in very fragmented areas, the longleaf pine forest is one of the most endangered ecosystems in North America.[12]

A longleaf pine forest is a unique ecological system. It shelters some of the most interesting and specialized plant communities in the world, such as the southeastern pitcher plant bog. This carnivorous plant–dominated wetland occurs just downslope from longleaf pine ridges, and these bogs are among the most biodiverse landscape systems on our continent.[13] But the longleaf pine region shelters many such diverse communities. Twenty-nine endangered or threatened animal species live within longleaf pine forests, and they harbor at least 122 species of threatened or endangered plants.[14] These specialized life forms are fine-tuned to the intricate characteristics that make a longleaf forest tick. Gopher tortoises (a land tortoise of ancient lineage) need occasional Piney Woods wildfires to stimulate the herbaceous plants and fruit that they consume. In the absence of fire, woody plants dominate the landscape and the gopher tortoises leave, in search of another place to live. Gopher tortoises are termed a keystone species, which means that hundreds of other species depend upon its existence. Up to 360 species of wildlife utilize the extensive tunnels that the threatened gopher tortoises dig.[15]

Other animals likewise depend on the continued existence of the longleaf pine forest. Federally endangered red-cockaded woodpeckers build their nests in the trunks of living, older pine trees. They drill holes in the trees with their bills so that the sticky tree sap will deter predators such as snakes. It has been observed that red-cockaded woodpeckers typically use trees that are at least sixty years old.[16] Since most forestry operations are on much shorter crop rotations, often less than thirty years, suitable red-cockaded pine habitat is now rare in the Southeast.

Longleaf pines take longer to grow than other pines. Today, most landowners and foresters tend to plant the quick-growing loblolly (*Pinus taeda*) or slash pine (*P. elliottii*). However, there has been a resurgence of planting longleaf pines in forestry operations. Numerous nonprofit groups have pledged to increase the longleaf pine range through various restoration activities. For instance, the staff at the Crosby Arboretum has replanted many longleaf pines in the Savanna Exhibit to better showcase this dwindling forest type.

Fire, usually thought of as destructor, gives birth to the Piney Woods landscape. Natural fires are caused by lightning, and lightning fires once burned frequently and unchecked through the lands. A study by J. M. Huffman assessed old pine stumps that contained abundant fire scars, concluding that wildfires have occurred regularly in five-year periods.[17] These frequent fires burned out the hardwood trees and underbrush, allowing dense carpets of grasses, wildflowers, and the fire-tolerant pines to flourish. Early explorers and colonists of the Gulf Coast found these open pine forests easy to travel in and hunt for game. Captain John Smith, the famous Jamestown settler, once wrote that "a man may gallop a horse amonst these woods any waie, but where the creeks and Rivers shall hinder."[18] W. C. Corsan, an English merchant who traveled at the time of the Civil War via rail from New Orleans to Jackson, Mississippi, noted the abundant open pine woods and magnificent rolling lands of southern Mississippi.[19]

In addition to lightning ignitions, fires were set in the landscape by indigenous peoples for many thousands of years. Tribes would use fire to open land up for better visibility, to clear fields for crops and agriculture, and for hunting purposes.[20] William Bartram, who traveled the southeastern United States in the 1770s, observed Native Americans setting the landscape on fire. He wrote in his *Travels through North and*

Fire was once a common landscape element in the Gulf Coast Piney Woods.

Photo courtesy of Crosby Arboretum

South Carolina, Georgia, East and West Florida, the Cherokee Country, etc. that fires occurred rather often, and "the trees and shrubs which cover these extensive wilds, are about five or six feet high, and seem to be kept down by the annual firing of the deserts."[21] While the frequency of the fires used by Native American tribes was highly variable, studies in the southern Appalachians show that fire was used by native cultures on average about every seven years.[22] Fire historian Stephen Pyne wrote that prescribed fire was probably used more in the Piney Woods region of the southeastern United States than anywhere else in the country.[23] Early herdsmen learned the Indian practice of using fire and with it helped to create vast grassy plains for livestock. Wildlife and fire-adapted plant species recover rapidly from occasional wildfires, and animal habitat and food availability increase with its use.[24]

Humans have been traced to the lands of the Gulf of Mexico for at least 12,000 years.[25] The coast must have been a very favorable place to live, with abundant fish and game populations, clean water, and, in some areas, good soils on which to grow crops. This region has always had a wealth of natural resources and a mild climate, and at one time it had a large Indian population. A Spanish expedition that landed near what is now the Mobile River in Alabama in 1519 noted forty nearby Indian settlements.[26] Hernando De Soto's expedition in 1539 observed that native peoples raised crops, burned their fields, cleared forests, and were well organized into towns and villages.[27]

On the ancestral lands of the Crosby Arboretum lived a tribal relative of today's Choctaw peoples called the Acolapissa.[28] The name of the now-extinct tribe stems from *okla pisa,* or those who "watch for people."[29] The Acolapissa lived at the mouth of the Pearl River and served as gatekeepers of the river that controlled access to the interior lands. In the early 1700s, French forts were established at Biloxi and military posts populated the lands. This was the first established European settlement of the region.[30] Jean-Baptiste Le Moyne de Bienville, the second French governor of Louisiana, noted in his journal that the Acolapissa along the Pearl River were very brave hunters.[31] Bienville mentioned that members of this tribe collected numerous small pearls from oysters found at the outlet of the Pearl River, although it has been written that the Pearl River received its name from the luster of the mussel shells that the Spaniards found along its banks.[32] As the British moved into the area in 1763 and the French left, the Acolapissa moved west above New Orleans.[33] It is believed that they eventually assimilated into the Houma Indian tribe, which still persists near New Orleans today. Choctaw tribes from the north then moved into the newly unoccupied lands along the Pearl River. But this was not for long; President Andrew Jackson's Indian Removal Act of 1830 forced most Native Americans east of the Mississippi River to abandon their ancestral homelands for territories in the West, leaving few in this region.[34]

When European settlers moved into Native territories in the early nineteenth century, they brought new ways of living and released cattle, horses, and hogs to range free on the land. Many of these emigrants were poor and unschooled, and they came to south Mississippi from the Carolinas and Georgia. They were different from the wealthy landowners that settled in other areas of Mississippi and that are typically associated with large plantations. The Natchez planters, for instance, were aristocratic and educated in the eastern United States, and mainly came from the Virginias.[35] Those that settled in south Mississippi were folks who farmed small plots and fished and hunted along the Pearl River.

These Piney Woods settlers learned how to use fire to improve and increase their rangeland, as fire brought forth tender grazing stems. Much of the uplands of the Gulf Coastal Plain contain poor mineral soils as compared to the richer bottomland areas, and farmers and landowners soon realized the value of burning off the stubble from last year's crop. Valuable nutrients that were locked up in stems and leaves were returned to the soil after a fire. Even today, much of the Piney Woods uplands are not known for good agricultural cropland, as the mostly mineral soils are better suited for timber production or pastureland.

South Mississippi grew slowly but steadily in the 1800s, with new towns being established along the Pearl River and Gulf Coast waterways. In 1841 the Pearl River was dredged to become navigable, and ports emerged along the river landings.[36] With development along the waterways, the interior forest lands remained sparsely populated and intact. John Francis Hamtranck Claiborne, a newspaper editor and U.S. representative, wrote about traveling through the south Mississippi landscape in the 1840s: "For twenty miles at a stretch you may ride through these ancient woods and see them as they have stood for countless years, untouched by the hand of man and only scratched by the lightning or the flying tempest. This growth of giant pines is unbroken on the route we pursued for a hundred miles or more, save where rivers or large water courses intervene." Claiborne forecast the events that would occur just fifty years later: "The time must arrive when this vast forest will become a source of value. The smoke of the steam mill will rise from a thousand hills. Rafts and lumber boats will sweep down the Pearl, the Leaf and Chickasawhay, and a railroad will transport millions of feet to the city of Mississippi to be shipped in vessels."[37]

Virgin longleaf pines in Mississippi were mostly harvested by the 1930s.

Photo courtesy of Crosby Arboretum

The late 1800s and early 1900s saw the largest wholesale removal of timber in the history of the southern United States, with significant environmental repercussions. Until the mid-nineteenth century, sawlogs were mainly cut near the rivers and floated downstream to lumber mills.[38] However, with the introduction of the locomotive in 1880, the forest interiors were wide open to harvest. Fifty years after the advent of railroads, the majority of Mississippi's attainable virgin timber on forested lands was cut. The timber industry in the state peaked in 1925 with over 3 billion board feet of harvested lumber.[39] Forestry operations were a massive industry, and two thirds of all industrial workers in the state were employed by lumber companies. Thousands of lumber camps and hundreds of small towns were hastily erected to house the workers of this booming economy. But just as fast as these hamlets were built, the trees were cut and hauled to nearby mills, and eventually only stumps remained. By the 1940s the majority of these small lumber settlements became ghost towns and would remain only as names on signs on lonely highways.

Despite these prior impacts from massive agriculture and forestry operations, the southeastern United States continues to harbor a rich supply of plant and animal species. This region is home to one of the most biologically diverse temperate forests in the world.[40] The abundance of water in the region creates a variety of aquatic environments, ranging from salt marsh estuaries to upland freshwater creeks. Subtle topographic changes and varied soil deposits also give rise to a wide range of vegetation types. Ten physiographic regions are found in Mississippi, including landscapes as diverse as the fall-line hills of the Appalachian Mountains, the alkaline black-belt prairie, and the loess hills along the Mississippi River floodplain.[41] The resulting tapestry of forest types includes numerous plant communities, such as upland longleaf pine forests, mesic (moist) pine-oak woodlands, hardwood bottomlands, and prairie meadows. These places house innumerable animal and plant species, some of which are found nowhere else.

Despite this biological richness, the Piney Woods ecosystem is still largely understudied and misunderstood. It is a complex and nuanced system of subtle gradients and environmental processes. The use of prescribed fire to manage grasslands is viewed skeptically by the public, locally and nationally.[42] Mississippi's wild lands are undervalued by its residents in part because of their abundance. Sixty-five percent of Mississippi's land mass is currently in forest.[43] A combination of plentiful natural wealth and a real need to boost local economies creates a perception that open lands are areas simply awaiting development. Urban sprawl is pervasive in the state, most noticeably around the larger cities of Jackson, Biloxi-Gulfport, and the northern border near Memphis, Tennessee.[44]

The rich cultural and natural history of south Mississippi and its surrounding region is pivotal to understanding the Crosby Arboretum. In fact, it is the reason why the Crosby Arboretum was born: to tell the story of the landscape and of the people who have lived there. The arboretum displays the plant communities of its ancestral past, allowing visitors to understand and appreciate the original landscape context. The geologic, biologic, and cultural stories embedded within the lands of the Crosby Arboretum are the very same narratives of Mississippi as a whole as well as its adjoining states. They share the same geologic history and have similar settlement patterns and land uses. In this way, the Crosby Arboretum is a microcosm of its region that tells the tale of its broader setting.

2

THE STORY

Having visited and studied botanic gardens and arboreta around the
world—from Buitenzorg to Guernsey—I have yet to experience one with
such a compelling mission, such design quality, or such a sensitively
conceived and well organized collection as found at the Crosby Arboretum.

—John O. Simonds, letter to Lynn Gammill, 1991

The Crosby Arboretum's history mirrors that of the greater landscape.
It is a story of the extraction of natural resources and of wrestling a living from an un-
forgiving land. As the Mississippi territories opened for purchase in the early 1800s,
speculators from faraway northern and eastern states bought large tracts of southern
lands. One such landowner from Michigan was John W. Blodgett, who held title to tens
of thousands of acres of pineland in Mississippi. In the early 1900s, a young entrepre-
neur named Lucius Olen Crosby and his partners made an offer to purchase Blodgett's
land. Blodgett agreed to "sell . . . you and your associates my tract of 42,316.13 acres in
Pearl River County, Mississippi . . . for the sum of \$3,385,000."[1] The time of the sale was
fortuitous, for the 1920s building boom in the midwestern United States demanded
enormous volumes of wood.[2] L. O. Crosby and the fledgling lumber and railroad town
of Picayune, Mississippi, flourished. The thirst for the extraction of yellow pine continued throughout south Mississippi, and within a few short decades only pine stumps
and abandoned lumber mills remained.

The tract of land that would one day become the Crosby Arboretum was clear-cut
of its vegetation by the 1930s.[3] Not one to sit on idle hands or lands, Crosby together
with his partners began to replant the cutover pine forest with a variety of farm crops.
Pine stumps were pulled from the ground by hard labor with oxen, and they were pro-

First shipment of strawberries from Crosby lands, March 1, 1932.

cessed at plants to make turpentine and tar.[4] Peaches, grapes, satsuma oranges, pecans, and tung trees were just a few of the orchard crops replanted in the eroded pine hills. The landscape once grew strawberries in the 1930s while the mill hands were idle. Ditches were dug in the wetland soils to make the land productive, and farm roads were built to transport the produce. These old agricultural ditches and roads are still readily visible on the Crosby Arboretum grounds.

The widespread loss of lumber jobs due to overharvesting and the Great Depression of the 1930s devastated workers and local economies. But Crosby's innovations and expansion into agriculture gave the people of Picayune much-needed employment. Longtime Crosby employee Freddie Acker reported that he worked in the Crosby strawberry fields as a young child and that he was able "to pick strawberries for 25 cents a day."[5]

By the start of World War II, L. O. Crosby had expanded his timber and agricultural industries to include chemical, creosote, wire-box plants, and tung nut production. In Pearl River County, over 100,000 acres were planted in tung trees (*Aleurites fordii*), making this county the tung capital of the world between 1937 and 1969.[6] Oil extracted from the tung nuts was used in paints and varnishes. When the elder Crosby's health failed, his three sons managed his interests. L. O. Crosby Jr. initiated some of the first forest restoration efforts in Mississippi. Most landowners at this time did not replant their harvested forest lands as they would be annually taxed if "improved." In 1939, Mississippi changed the tax system to a severance type so that crops were not taxed until harvested.[7] This allowed timber owners to replant their stump-lands without the burden of additional taxation.

The Strawberry Farm, as the site of the Crosby Arboretum was then known, was planted in slash pines sometime in the 1940s and managed thereafter as a pine plantation. This first crop of pines would never be harvested, for in 1969 a category 5 hurricane leveled the pine forests of Pearl River County and surrounding regions. Hurricane Camille resulted in 259 deaths in four states.[8] The former Strawberry Farm was in the storm's direct path and lost much timber, yet a fair number of those planted pine trees exist today. Prior to Hurricane Camille, another change would occur, as the original 640-acre Strawberry Farm was split by Interstate 59 along its eastern edge. This cut created a leftover piece of 64 acres filled with a remnant patch of pine trees. This area would eventually become the Interpretive Center of the Crosby Arboretum.

THE IDEA

After a long and successful career in timber and other industries, L. O. Crosby Jr. passed away on Christmas Eve 1978.[9] His family, including his wife Dorothy and two children, L. O. Crosby III and Lynn Gammill, and son-in-law Stewart Gammill III, immediately began considering a memorial. As the family traveled to Picayune on the interstate, they drove past the old Strawberry Farm and thought about creating a place in his memory that might honor his love of the outdoors. L. O. Crosby III (Osmond) ventured, "Well, what about if it had something to do with every kind of tree?" Since the family was most familiar with the timber business, they admittedly knew little about creating memorial gardens. A family friend suggested building an arboretum, but as Lynn Gammill noted, "we had to look up what an arboretum was in a dictionary."[10] They began by forming a board of directors between the years 1979 and 1981 and looked to Mississippi State University (MSU) for assistance. Lynn and Stewart Gammill had previously worked with the MSU Department of Forestry regarding some business on forest lands. George Switzer, professor of forestry, and William Giles, president emeritus of MSU, were included as the first board members.

Selecting an arboretum site was a primary concern. An early board member who would eventually become the Crosby Arboretum's first registrar was Katherine Moak Furr. Mrs. Furr was a longtime friend of the Crosby family and would be instrumental in building community support for the young facility. Furr's cousin, Mary Hough, was another important community liaison. Mrs. Hough worked in the County Extension office and actively recruited volunteers to assist in arboretum activities. Katherine Furr recalled that in the early 1980s the board members "drove around and around looking for a suitable place" to build the arboretum.[11] While there were numerous picturesque areas on Crosby properties that could have been selected, the family decided that the old Strawberry Farm would be the best location. It was the site of their father's first pine replanting efforts and was readily accessible from the interstate. Board member Switzer had reservations about the site and advocated for a place that was not as heavily disturbed by agriculture and forestry.[12] But the board selected the Strawberry Farm, where the Crosby legacy was strong.

As the idea for the Crosby Arboretum grew, founder Lynn Gammill recalled, "We began to realize what it took to build an Arboretum, and we knew we needed a landscape architect and an architect. Through Dr. Giles and Dr. Switzer we met Ed Blake."[13] Edward L. Blake Jr. (also called "Ned") taught in the Department of Landscape Architecture at MSU and was an early arboretum consultant. Blake had a keen appreciation for the Mississippi landscape and had assisted his father on the design of trails at the family's Christmas tree farm in Pocahontas, Mississippi. When Blake first saw the proposed arboretum property in 1980, it had just been burned to control the underbrush, and the site had little more to offer than struggling pine trees and a blackened landscape. He said to himself, "What on earth can we do here?"[14]

Lynn Gammill noted that the board of directors remained open to options and explorations of the general concept: "The early board was more of a think-tank board, and not constrained from thinking out loud. A lot was done at the lodge and you think differently when you are in nature."[15] The lodge that Mrs. Gammill referred to was Little Black Creek Lodge, a family retreat set on the banks of a small creek in the middle of a managed longleaf pine plantation. The Crosby board and consultants would frequently meet there to discuss their plans.

The board of directors expanded to include prominent friends and family, who thought it prudent to visit and observe other notable gardens and arboreta in the United States and abroad. Board members needed to learn about the many details of establishing an arboretum, and were interested in children's gardens and educational programs. Early board member Jean du Pont Blair was related to the du Pont family that had established several notable gardens near Philadelphia. Jean and the other board members traveled in the early 1980s to Longwood Gardens, Winterthur, and other gardens in the Brandywine Valley of southeastern Pennsylvania and northern Delaware.[16] The quality and variety of the gardens they encountered caused one board member, Jean Chisholm Lindsey, to remark that there were already enough great gardens around and that "it's already been done."[17]

But these garden visits put the board members in touch with leading horticultural experts that provided valuable advice. Fred Galle, then director of horticulture at Callaway Gardens in Georgia, was an early consultant to the Crosby board, as was Dr. Neil Odenwald, who was professor of landscape architecture at Louisiana State University.[18] An influential adviser was Dr. Richard Lighty, a botanist at Longwood Gardens and director of Mt. Cuba Center for the Study of Piedmont Flora in Greenville, Delaware. It was Lighty who told the visiting board members that indeed the great

Consultants and members of the first board of directors of the Crosby Arboretum include, from left, Sidney McDaniel, project botanist; William Ferris; George Switzer; William Giles; Edward L. Blake Jr.; Jean du Pont Blair; Hap Owen; Katherine Furr; Richard Cowart; Dorothy Crosby; L. O. Crosby III; Lynn Gammill; and Stewart Gammill; early 1980s.

Photo courtesy of Crosby Arboretum

garden styles from Europe had already been implemented in America, and that the board should instead consider "looking at the plants of their own backyard."[19] He emphasized that the Crosby Arboretum could feature the native plants of their region. Don Hendricks, director of Dawes Arboretum in Newark, Ohio, gave similar advice.[20] The board would eventually rally around this idea and incorporate it into the arboretum's initial mission statement.[21]

Ed Blake also traveled extensively to public arboreta, and he observed how gardens displayed the native plants of their region. He noted that the Brandywine Conservancy in Pennsylvania "made excellent use of indigenous materials" and that he liked the Cary Arboretum in New York for its "method of working with native materials in a very natural setting."[22] These observations of other facilities would influence many of the design solutions utilized in the Crosby Arboretum Master Plan.

Considering the many land-use changes occurring in Mississippi, Dr. George Switzer wrote in a 1983 article: "With all the change our society is experiencing today, the bulk of the populace tends to get detached from the natural aspects of the landscape.

I foresee a greater need for such preservation as the Arboretum is involved with in the future."[23] Little did Dr. Switzer know that this human detachment from nature would increase over time and eventually become known as "nature deficit disorder."[24] Board member Giles echoed the need for a greater understanding of local ecology: "The major contribution of the Crosby Arboretum is an educational one, and for the first time the flora of a sizeable region in Mississippi will be presented to the public."[25] Giles also recognized that a native arboretum could serve to teach people about native plants via gardening and landscape topics.

The potential cost savings of establishing and maintaining a native plant garden versus a traditionally planted arboretum of exotics was appealing to the board. Lynn Gammill wrote in the 1983 Crosby Arboretum *News Journal:* "Older, established arboreta that maintain formal displays spend a great deal of time and money just for upkeep. We feel that through more natural displays, the Crosby Arboretum can better concentrate its resources on educational programs that stress the significance of ecological interrelationships."[26] The Crosby Arboretum was not endowed by the Crosby family for its funding and perpetual management, so the decision to use the services provided by nature was not only unique at the time in the botanic world, but profound. Very few garden facilities in the early 1980s were using ecologically based design to guide their exhibit structure and maintenance. The Crosby founders would espouse one other important guiding principle, to "do a few things, but do them well."[27]

Although the arboretum directors were advised to focus on Mississippi's ecology and native plants, the Crosby family's attention to history and Mississippi culture would ensure an important melding of the arts and the sciences. In particular, Lynn Gammill's interests in American history and community arts would play an important role in forging a strong cultural expression, in addition to a natural one, for the arboretum. This interplay between culture and nature would become the philosophical foundation for the facility and would heighten its ultimate expressions of architecture, programs, and interpretation. But first, the Crosby Arboretum founders needed to better understand the landscape they sought to showcase by studying its physical and biological characteristics.

THE LAND

Forced to look, led to observe, one suddenly sees, as through new eyes, a world of beauty in the most ordinary things.

—Teiji Ito and Takeji Iwanya, *The Japanese Garden* (1978)

The entire Interpretive Center site in 1982 was open pine forest.

Photo courtesy of Crosby Arboretum

In the early 1980s, the Crosby Arboretum site was a remnant pine plantation that still bore the scars of the old Strawberry Farm. Other than ditches and dirt roads, the primary landscape features were scattered slash and loblolly trees planted in the 1940s. Waves of grasses and abundant wildflowers were in the dense understory. Trucks and cars passing on adjacent Interstate 59 were easily seen and heard across much of the property. It was a daunting place to build a public garden.

The connection to MSU strengthened in the early days of the Crosby Arboretum, when Dr. Sidney McDaniel joined the team. McDaniel was a professor of biology at MSU and one of the best field botanists in Mississippi. He knew the Coastal Plain landscape and understood its changing and dynamic nature. McDaniel was retained as a consultant to the project, and he established a herbarium of the plants found on the Crosby Arboretum site.

A physical survey of the property and its topographic features gave the designers and biologists a base plan to work upon. But a 64-acre facility is a large place to conduct a comprehensive survey of all the plants. The Crosby board contacted other botanic garden administrators for information on establishing an arboretum, and Don Hendricks of the Dawes Arboretum again provided key advice. He suggested that Crosby place geographic markers inside the arboretum to become permanent reference points.[28] These reference markers would framework the entire site into a grid of one-hundred-foot-square plots that could be individually studied. Brass stakes were tamped into the ground at each corner of the grid sections. At the top of each stake was placed a brass plate stamped with the unique identifiers for that location. In addition to becoming permanent reference markers for subsequent floristic surveys, the brass markers became key alignment points for the locations of structures in the arboretum's Master Plan. Dr. McDaniel noted that "the grid system is the primary way of identifying and locating [plant] specimens on the site. I laid out the grid system on the site, inventoried and catalogued plants on the site, investigated possible natural areas, and did vegetation studies for the natural areas."[29]

Data collection on the previous Strawberry Farm site began in earnest within the first few years of selecting the arboretum's location. A thorough understanding of the landscape and its workings would later prove invaluable in the design and layout of the Master Plan. Dr. McDaniel and others classified this area as a wet pine flatwood prior to being farmed in the 1930s. Pine flatwoods range from Florida to Louisiana and are common landscape features along the Gulf Coast. More accurately known as the East Gulf Coastal Plain near-coast pine flatwoods, these landscapes have low, flat land and poorly drained soils. The arboretum's original landscape was most likely a mix of pine savanna and hardwood thickets. Fires would have swept across the landscape in dry periods, and the region's ample moisture levels ensured dense and rampant shrub growth. These are usually not the ideal environmental conditions in which to establish an arboretum.

The nearly level landscape of pine flatwoods is likely the remnant of ancient floodplains. These floodplains drop silts and clays from their stagnant, murky waters, which build the soil up in thick layers. Soils sampled on the Crosby Arboretum site are mainly silts and clays, and include the Escambia, Smithton, and Atmore series.[30] The poorly drained Smithton and Atmore soils are found in the drainageways and are commonly associated with wetland shrubs such as titi (*Cyrilla racemiflora*), wax myrtle (*Morella cerifera*), and saw palmetto (*Serenoa repens*).[31] These are found primarily in the center of the arboretum site.

Escambia soils are found on the slightly higher rises at the eastern edge of the site and are associated with dryland tree species, such as longleaf pine, gallberry (*Ilex glabra*), and wiregrass (*Aristida stricta*).[32] As evidenced from soil borings taken in 1983, far below these soil types are deep layers of sand, which suggest that this area was once part of a much faster and dynamic river system. These soil types govern the types of plants that can best perform at the arboretum. The heavy presence of wetland soils would have presented an obstacle to more traditional garden approaches on this site without significant horticultural and landscape interventions. But incorporating wetland plants and communities was deemed appropriate to this particular landscape.

Because of the fine-textured soils and the region's significant rainfall, standing water is a common feature of the Crosby Arboretum property. After a heavy rain, water drains across the arboretum as a sheetflow, similar to how water in the Everglades National Park flows in a broad, shallow pattern. Occasionally, rainfalls can cause four to six inches of water to flood much of the arboretum site, but it rapidly drains offsite. The arboretum landscape is riddled with agricultural ditches from its prior farm days, which mainly flow toward the center of the property.

The soils here also feature a perched water table that keeps the groundwater close to the surface. A dense clay layer in the soil at six feet below the ground prevents water penetration. Similar to a bathtub, water collects on top of this impermeable soil layer and builds to the surface in the winter months. In summer, because of drought and tree evapotranspiration, the water table drops to lower levels. Owing to these seasonally wet conditions, ephemeral (short-duration) wetlands are fairly common features in the region.

It is these abundant wetlands that give rise to the amazing biodiversity in the Gulf South's plant communities. Cypress swamps, pitcher plant bogs, gum ponds, and bottomland hardwoods are some of the interesting landscapes along the river basins. The region's humid subtropical climate allows for the natural occurrence of fascinating and visually striking plants, such as dwarf palmetto (*Sabal minor*), agave (*Agave americana*), and native hibiscus (*Hibiscus* spp.). Tangled masses of vines stretch into the tree canopies, which can resemble the liana forests of Central America and South America. The wildlife in these south Mississippi forests appears just as exotic and unworldly as the plants: bright green anole lizards jump from trunk to tree limb, and great blue herons stretch their wingtips to a full-grown man's height. South Mississippi landscapes appear to have sprung from the primordial soup of life.

As the botanists were collecting plant species data from the arboretum site, the early board wrestled with the concept of the mission statement. What is a regional plant arboretum, and what would it look like? Although many other arboreta and botanic gardens featured native plants or had wild places as part of their holdings, few at that time embodied a comprehensive plant community concept for their entire facility. Board member Osmond Crosby tells the story of his visit to the Muttart Conservatory in Edmonton, Alberta, which features plants from various parts of the world. The plant collections are encased in pyramidal glass enclosures. He recalls seeing an indoor exhibit on lower Coastal Plain plants that was interesting, "but there were a couple of pitcher plants that were basically on life support. They were very spindly and sickly. It was at that point that I had the epiphany that devoting massive resources to keeping plants barely alive was not a good idea. It fits into the concept that we didn't want to be another botanical garden with plants from the Northwest or Orient on display in the South."[33]

A regional arboretum would require, first, that the board define the scope of its region. This question would persist well into 1987, when discussions were still occurring of focusing the Crosby Arboretum on a much broader exhibit concept—perhaps featuring landscape types from the entire Gulf Coastal Plain. The directors decided to concentrate the arboretum's efforts on the Pearl River watershed. The Pearl is a major 444-mile-long river that runs in a north-south direction through the state of Mississippi, roughly paralleling the Mississippi River located to its west. The Pearl originates near the geographic center of Mississippi, and its lower portion serves as the boundary line between Mississippi and Louisiana. Eventually, the Pearl releases into the Gulf of Mexico. The rainwater from the arboretum site drains within a few short miles into the eastern branch of the Pearl River. Eventually, the board would settle on the following Crosby Arboretum mission statement: to be "a regional Arboretum representing the native flora of the Pearl River drainage basin in Mississippi and Louisiana."[34]

By including native flora in its mission statement, the arboretum had placed high value upon its region's genetic material. This sentiment was being echoed increasingly in the 1980s as the world witnessed a rapid degradation of biological diversity. Michael Pollan wrote in *Second Nature* (1991): "If you think of evolution as the three-and-a-half-billion-year-long laboratory experiment, and the gene pool as the store of information accumulated during the course of the experiment, you begin to appreciate that nature has far more extensive knowledge about her operations than we do."[35] By conserving local native material, the Crosby Arboretum would preserve its region's genetic legacy.

Equally important in the arboretum's discussion of place and biological heritage was Mississippi's culture. Influencing this was University of Southern Mississippi English professor Noel Polk, who edited a book of essays entitled *Mississippi's Piney Woods: A Human Perspective*. This book defined the cultural history of the Piney Woods and its identity with a distinct sense of place. William Ferris, director of the University of Mississippi's Center for the Study of Southern Culture, was also an early Crosby Arboretum consultant. The center's mission was to document and study Mississippi's culture for academic and public interests.[36] As Mississippi was being swept into the increased globalization of the twentieth century, southern culture and its characteristic customs, language, and cooking were rapidly changing. While cultural attributes were not specified in Crosby Arboretum's mission statement, the facility would make room for local people and their historical interactions within the Piney Woods landscape, and cultural heritage preservation would become a subset of the arboretum's mission.[37] This celebration of traditional cultural knowledge is still preserved in the arboretum's annual Piney Woods Heritage Festival.

CROSBY ARBORETUM NATURAL AREAS

Dr. Sidney McDaniel and his graduate student Christopher J. Wells inventoried the first plant species data of the Crosby Arboretum site and began a collection of the specimens. This led to the establishment of the arboretum's herbarium collection in 1984, which was further developed by Wells. After earning his graduate degree in biology from MSU, Wells would become the arboretum's first employee, hired as the superintendent of arboretum lands. His initial tasks included digging wells to observe changes in the groundwater table, collecting soil samples, collecting and identifying plant species, and propagating plants.[38] The arboretum planners and board members quickly realized that the 64-acre site was too small to fully achieve their mission statement of conserving and displaying the plant communities representing an 8,700-square-mile watershed basin.

In 1984, the planners conceived that the arboretum could incorporate satellite natural areas in addition to the 64-acre memorial public garden.[39] A few arboreta in the nation already included natural areas as part of their holdings, including the University of Wisconsin Arboretum and the Missouri Botanic Garden, but this was still not a commonly accepted idea. The natural areas would not only be conserved for their intact plant communities but also would function as research locations to inspire the design for the Interpretive Center, and for occasional visitation by the public. The Crosby forestry land holdings already contained a wealth of diverse plant community habitats, and many of these were located within an hour's driving distance of the Interpretive Center. Ed Blake recorded in his notebook that "rather than a museum collection of plants, the [Crosby] Arboretum was to become a museum of place."[40]

After touring many of the Crosby timber lands, Dr. McDaniel readily identified distinct examples of Piney Woods plant communities that could become part of the arboretum's holdings. These included a wide range of upland and bottomland habitats as well as the floodplains of small or medium-sized rivers and creeks. Very few were picturesque landscapes that would inspire awe in the viewer. There were no mountains or waterfalls, but these were instead excellent representations of locally occurring plant habitats. These habitats included pitcher plant bogs, shrub bogs, bottomland hardwoods, and longleaf pine ridges. The plant communities that were identified on Crosby timber lands were simply set aside as natural areas under a verbal lease agreement with Crosby family members. Two natural areas, Mill Creek and Hillside Bog, were purchased by the arboretum board.

These natural areas became the conservatories of the arboretum, and the 64-acre native plant center in Picayune, the old Strawberry Farm, would become the Interpretive Center. In this way, the interpretive site would be built to handle visitors and their needs while the natural areas would remain undeveloped and little impacted. The interpretive site would showcase examples of plant communities as compressed landscapes found within the natural areas so that after a short walk around the arboretum, visitors would see and learn about their regional landscape. The Interpretive Center would become the public lens through which the complex interactions of the natural areas would be displayed and discussed.

The natural area concept was ratified by the arboretum board, and by 1987 the Crosby Arboretum maintained 1,700 acres on eleven separate sites. These natural area holdings would eventually reduce in size to the current figure of 700 acres on seven separate sites. This reduction in acreage occurred as some natural areas became part of U.S. Fish and Wildlife Service lands, and the others were dissociated because of accessibility or management concerns.

Research was paramount to the formation of the Crosby Arboretum collections. Dr. McDaniel expertly summarized the general landscape patterns of the lower Coastal Plain in a simple graph. In their most basic form, the various plant communities of the Pearl River basin are largely shaped by two environmental factors: the amount of moisture present in the soil and the occurrence of fire. Available sunlight increases in an area after a wildfire or after a hurricane or tornado removes trees.

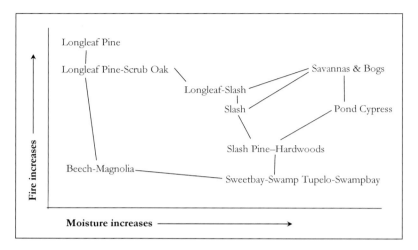

This graph displays the Gulf Coast plant communities that naturally form due to the influences of fire and soil moisture. These community types are found in Crosby Arboretum natural areas and helped give shape to the arboretum's exhibits.

Original graph by Dr. Sidney McDaniel, redrawn by the author

The increased sunlight causes sun-loving plants to repopulate an area that was once shaded woodland. Similarly, plants are adapted to certain ranges of moisture conditions. According to the graph of plant community relations as devised by Dr. McDaniel, longleaf pine forests tend to occur where there is periodic fire and on higher elevations (minimal soil moisture). Alternately, beech-magnolia forests are typically found in the absence of fire in older woodlands on higher elevations (moist soils). Plants that are adapted to much wetter conditions are not found within these drier forest types. Thus the different plant community types respond to the major environmental factors to which they are best adapted.

Each distinct plant community also has an ecotone, or a zone where it meets another plant community. For example, when a fire-maintained grassland savanna abuts a shaded forest, there is a transition zone of dense shrubs and trees that take advantage of the extra light until it is too shady for them to live. These ecotones are the gradation zones between two distinctly different communities.

The acquisition of the natural areas was a significant accomplishment of the Crosby Arboretum, and they became valuable sites that would influence the design and development of the Interpretive Center. The following is a list of the current Crosby Arboretum natural areas and their descriptions:[41]

HILLSIDE BOG. This bog (a wet, spongy ground) is known for its sweeping hillside vista of pitcher plants. Consisting of nearly seventy acres in Hancock County, this natural area was purchased by the Crosby Arboretum with the assistance of the Nature Conservancy. The name refers to the fact that the pitcher bog occurs on the lower

Hillside Bog features several breath-taking acres of yellow pitcher plants and their associated bog species.

Photo courtesy of Crosby Arboretum

slope of the hillside. Most bogs occur in the lowest elevation of a drain swale and not on the slopes of hills. At Hillside, however, a perched water table keeps the groundwater at a higher level. In addition to the vast pitcher plant habitat, Hillside Bog harbors a longleaf pine ridge, a sweetbay–swamp tupelo–swampbay (wet woodland) community, and a beautiful blackwater stream (blackwater refers to the dark color of the creek water due to a high organic content). A rare giant orchid (*Pteroglossaspis ecristata*) occurs in the longleaf pine area.

Hillside Bog is maintained through regular applications of prescribed fire. It is best visited in early spring when the unusual chartreuse "buttercup" flowers of the pitcher plant dominate the ground layer. These are followed by the bright green tubes of the pitcher plant leaves, which trap insects as they slip inside. There are many hundreds of thousands of pitcher plants at Hillside Bog, packed densely together. Pitcher plants expand by rhizomes (lateral roots), which creep out from the center of the clump. Because pitchers grow slowly, Hillside Bog must be very old.

Several other types of carnivorous plants occur here, including parrot's pitcher plant (*Sarracenia psittacina*), red sundew (*Drosera brevifolia*), and buttercup (*Pinquicula* sp.). Fall is another time of interest, when numerous wildflowers such as swamp sunflower (*Helianthus angustifolius*), liatris (*Liatris* sp.), and thoroughworts (*Eupatorium* sp.) erupt in a colorful meadow display. In late fall, the misty mornings create dreamscapes of longleaf pine silhouettes undergirded by dewy wiregrass (*Aristida* sp.).

DEAD TIGER CREEK HAMMOCK. While no one knows how Dead Tiger Creek received its name, the term *hammock* refers to a low, nonalluvial (not formed from a river) hardwood swamp. Hammocks are found throughout the Gulf Coastal Plain and Florida, but Dead Tiger Creek Hammock is one of the westernmost hammocks in the southeastern United States. This flooded landscape is mostly an impenetrable shrub thicket that harbors some interesting plant species. Pink coreopsis (*Coreopsis nudata*) and flameflower (*Macranthera flammea*) are rare wildflowers that have been found here.

Winter is the best time to visit the hammock. At this time of year, most of the leaves have fallen from the shrubs, allowing for easier access. Most important, during winter the plentiful cottonmouth snakes are hibernating. This dense, twisted landscape is thick in wetland shrubs and trees, including pond cypress (*Taxodium ascendens*), titi, and sweetbay magnolia (*Magnolia virginiana*). Fire does not commonly occur in this perennially wet landscape.

DEAD TIGER CREEK SAVANNA. This 20-acre natural area contains an upland longleaf pine ridge, a hillside bog, and a wet savanna. It is located within a mile of Dead Tiger Creek Hammock, and its small drainage channels feed directly into the hammock. Pine lily (*Lilium catesbaei*) and several types of pitcher plants (*Sarracenia*) are found here. This landscape is also maintained by regular applications of prescribed fire. Fire tends to promote the dominance of grasses and wildflowers except near the wetter portions, which exhibit more vines and shrubs.

RED BLUFF. Red Bluff is the largest of Crosby's natural areas and encompasses approximately 320 acres of land. The land surrounds a broad blackwater stream named

Catahoula Creek. This area is a part of the Stennis Space Center buffer zone, where structures of any type (housing or commercial) are not allowed due to possible damage. The natural area is connected to several thousand acres of natural lands owned by the federal government. Red Bluff contains a wealth of environments including oxbow lakes (abandoned river channels), pine woods, and gum swamps. A nearby horse rental facility often uses the creek and roads for trails. Interesting plants include saw palmetto, Georgia calaminth (*Clinopodium georgianum*), and wild olive (*Osmanthus americanus*).

TALOWAH. This natural area consists of 120 acres of longleaf pine ridges and creek bottoms in Pearl River County. Talowah was a magnificent site when the arboretum first leased the land from the Crosby family. It was one of the oldest longleaf pine stands in the county, estimated at that time to be about ninety years old. Unfortu-

Talowah features upland longleaf pine forests interspersed with stream corridors, circa 1980s.

nately, Hurricane Katrina in 2005 and logging returned most of the site to an earlier age. Due to the frequent burning, many composites and legumes occur in the upland areas, while ferns and sedges are found in lower hardwoods. A rare grass called Apalachicola Indiangrass (*Sorghastrum apalachicolense*) has been found here.

MILL CREEK. Just twenty acres in size, Mill Creek Natural Area is found along the edge of a small branch of the East Pearl River. Although Hurricane Katrina caused much damage to the site, it is still predominantly a beech-magnolia woodland. Beech trees a century in age or older are found in clusters, and the charming pink flowers of native azaleas (*Rhododendron canescens*) and mountain laurel (*Kalmia latifolia*) line the creek terraces. Five species of magnolias occur, as well as alternate-leaved dogwood (*Cornus alternifolia*) and the magnificent wild camellia (*Stewartia malacodendron*).

STEEP HOLLOW. About 110 acres in extent, Steep Hollow contains a quaking bog (a floating mat of peat that shakes when walked upon), longleaf pine slopes and ridges, and a sweetbay–tupelo–swampbay bottomland. Quaking bogs form in the valleys between the upland pine ridges and often develop a deep, saturated peat layer. This area contains rare plant species including bog spicebush (*Lindera subcoriacea*), bog flax (*Linum macrocarpum*), white arrow arum (*Peltandra sagittifolia*), coastal sedge (*Carex exilis*), and Indiangrass.

The acquisition of the Crosby Arboretum natural areas was important for the cataloging of the plants and plant communities of the lower Gulf Coast. Biologists from across the southeastern United States have conducted studies on these lands and confirmed their biological interest and value. Tours with limited numbers of visitors are conducted at these natural areas through the Crosby Arboretum's regular program schedule, but the areas are mainly utilized for research and conservation purposes. Visitors learn about the natural areas through an introductory film at the Interpretive Center that features their plants and plant communities.

PERMANENT RESEARCH PLOTS

The natural areas serve as living references for the plant accessioning and diversity efforts at the Interpretive Center. While the natural areas exist mainly for research, the Interpretive Center was planted and heavily manipulated to showcase the plant community displays for visitors. In 1989, the Crosby Arboretum received a grant from the federal Institute of Museum Services to establish research plots in each natural area of the arboretum and to conduct vegetation surveys.[42] Arboretum botanist Chris Wells selected sections for research plots in each natural area that contained similar environments at the 64-acre visitors' site.

The establishment of permanent plots and their subsequent studies at the natural areas allowed for better-informed design and management decisions at the Interpretive Center. The list of plants generated from the natural areas' research formed the basis of the proposed species to be planted within the arboretum's exhibits. But there was still an uncertainty among the board members about how to incorporate native plants into the Interpretive Center, and they were equally unsure of the aesthetics of the resulting design. The board's visits to other arboreta and botanic gardens brought them to the opinion that they did not want to feature native plants in a horticultural setting, but instead to explore some greater partnership with nature. The Crosby Arboretum would focus less on displays of horticultural "products" such as the particular species or unique cultivars found elsewhere, and would instead feature how the processes of nature shape resulting plant communities. This was a revolutionary thought in the world of arboreta at the time, when many of the leading botanic gardens, landscape architects, biologists, and the visiting public drew a distinct and heavy line between gardens and nature. The main question yet to be resolved at the Crosby Arboretum was this: how does one succeed if there are few precedents from which to learn?

3

THE GENESIS OF THE CROSBY ARBORETUM

Gardens are the link between men and the world in which they live,
for men in every age have felt the need to reconcile themselves with
their surroundings, and have created gardens to satisfy their ideals and
aspirations.

—Sylvia Crowe, *Garden Design*

The earliest humans were inspired by nature. This is evident from the first simple yet striking cave drawings at Lascaux, France, and the touching remnants of cut flowers placed in Neanderthal graves: there is enduring evidence of people evoking nature.[1] We are instinctively drawn to our world's lushness and its healing qualities upon the soul. For we come from, and are, nature.

Cultures throughout time have viewed their surroundings through the lens of their own cosmologies. One common thread that is woven throughout the fabric of humanity is the garden as metaphor for the larger world or universe. During the Han dynasty of the second century BCE, a garden was arranged to symbolize a microcosm of the rest of the world.[2] Even in early Western cultures, the garden was viewed as a link between the physical and spiritual needs of people, and emerged as humankind's ideal of an earthly paradise. The books of the Old Testament use the words "garden," "park," and "paradise" interchangeably.

But with these cultural distinctions, nature was often displayed as a pictorial artifact in the garden, instead of a living ecological area. In tenth-century China, garden designers utilized paintings to influence their garden designs.[3] Chinese painters from this period abstracted the natural landscape using rocks, trees, and water arranged into visual compositions. These paintings influenced garden designers, who also created two-dimensional settings to be viewed from certain vantages. These arrangements were artfully abstracted into the garden with little concern of how they functioned ecologically.

In the fifteenth and sixteenth centuries, European travelers to China brought landscape paintings back to Europe, inspiring Western garden designers. The Taoist philosophy embodied in these paintings conveyed a relationship with nature that deeply impressed European artists. Landscape paintings soon became commonplace as the technical skills of the Western artist improved. These landscape depictions further idealized the forms and aesthetics of nature.[4] The seventeenth-century paintings of Nicolas Poussin, Claude Lorrain, and Salvator Rosa profoundly affected garden designers, who tried to simulate the pictorial compositions of these paintings in their garden designs.

In the eighteenth century, William Kent, Capability Brown, and Humphry Repton founded the English Gardening School, which also espoused the creation of pictorial idealizations of nature in garden design. These designs were scenic representations meant to be observed from certain locations within the garden. In America, Frederick Law Olmsted, the landscape designer of Central Park in New York City and father of the profession of landscape architecture, was influenced by the pastoral English landscape and the Gardening School. Olmsted and his partner, Calvert Vaux, used a naturalistic style that took advantage of natural features and scenery in picturesque landscape compositions.

To counter the more formal garden styles of the day, America in the late nineteenth century saw a popular rise in the notion of the "wild garden."[5] Many magazines at the time featured articles on wildflowers and conservation of the wilderness. English gardener William Robinson was an early advocate of naturalizing plant species, both exotic and native, in the landscape. In his 1873 book, *The Wild Garden,* he recommends using native plants in the garden as they are observed in nature.

In the early to mid-twentieth century, a few American environmentalists developed key ideas regarding human interpretations of nature. One was Aldo Leopold, a scientist and forester who wrote *A Sand County Almanac* in 1949. There he maintains that people have a land ethic, or an inherent responsibility to protect and care for the land they live on. *A Sand County Almanac* was a landmark book that would influence the thoughts and writings of subsequent generations.

While the prevailing modernist movement held sway in much of the arts, landscape, and architecture world in the early twentieth century, a few designers sought instead their own regional landscape expressions. Landscape architect Jens Jensen, who lived in the Chicago area, developed the Prairie Landscape style. Jensen explored an abstraction of the region's predominant historic landscape type in his designs for parks and private estates, and was an early advocate of ecological restoration. Other early communicators espousing the use of ecology in garden design were Elsa Rehmann and Edith Roberts. Roberts was a professor of botany at Vassar College, and Rehmann was one of the first women landscape architects. Their books, which include *American Plants for American Gardens,* and their magazine articles from the 1920s propose using native plant community themes in gardens and landscaping.[6] Rehmann and Roberts were among the first to promote ecological landscaping in the popular press.

But it would take the environmental movement of the 1960s to foster dramatic changes in public consciousness and in the landscape world. According to Stewart Udall, then secretary of the interior under the Kennedy administration, the environmental revolution of the 1970s was caused by three seminal books: Rachel Carson's *Silent Spring,* Leopold's *A Sand County Almanac,* and Ian McHarg's *Design with Nature.*[7]

With the notable exception of the University of Pennsylvania's program, academic programs in landscape architecture in the 1960s were slow to embrace and teach ecological concepts. Led by its charismatic leader, Ian McHarg, Penn's program soon became internationally known for its focus on ecological planning. McHarg understood the landscape as a process, not a product, and emphasized how planning must adapt to a living environment.[8] His *Design with Nature* (1969) influenced generations of planners and landscape architects and continues to shape analytical environmental planning today. McHarg called for planning and design to create symbiotic environments for both people and the planet. He passionately portrayed his concept of ecological planning as the best option for society, its economics, and the environment.

In addition to his teaching duties at the University of Pennsylvania, McHarg was a partner in the landscape planning firm of Wallace, McHarg, Roberts & Todd (WMRT). Here, McHarg could apply his environmental planning ideas through implementation and testing in the real world. Two young couples who worked for McHarg at WMRT were also his former students, Carol and Colin Franklin, and Leslie and Rolf Sauer. Their combined backgrounds of landscape architecture, architecture, biology, and engineering made a complete professional unit, and together they would leave WMRT and form the Philadelphia-based landscape architecture and planning firm Andropogon Associates in 1975.[9]

Espousing McHarg's teaching and ideals, Andropogon completed work for a number of parklands and arboreta and earned a reputation for using native plant materials and communities. In 1983 Bill Klein, then director of the Morris Arboretum, introduced Crosby Arboretum master planner Edward Blake to Andropogon's Leslie Sauer.[10] At that time, the Crosby board of directors was searching for the best consultants to steer the Master Plan process. Andropogon Associates not only came highly recommended, but also was one of the few firms with experience in ecologically designed systems. McHarg noted in his book *A Quest for Life* (1997) that despite his impassioned efforts, very few landscape architects were working with ecological systems. He could name only three—Jones and Jones (Seattle), Coe Lee Robinson Roesch (Philadelphia), and Andropogon. While McHarg was a prophet of the 1960s environmental wave, the timing was too far in advance for most people to embrace these concepts in their own backyards.

EARLY CROSBY ARBORETUM MASTER PLANS

In today's zoos we see a trend away from the pachyderm or feline house toward the African plains and northern woods exhibits. Similarly, arboreta are beginning to develop the habitat display as a setting for their collections, such as the pine sand hills at the University of North Carolina Arboretum. This approach is somewhat new and still evolving as a design style. However, designing with nature is not, as it is sometimes assumed to be, no design at all or merely "naturalistic." Based on natural models and respectful of natural processes, this design approach seeks to forge a new relationship between the viewer and the native landscape, which is emotionally and aesthetically satisfying as well as educational.

—Andropogon Associates, "Outline for Developing the First-Year Program of the Crosby Arboretum," 1983

Ed Blake at the Crosby Arboretum.

Photo courtesy of Crosby Arboretum

At first, the Crosby founders thought it a relatively simple task to create a Master Plan for the arboretum. After all, Ed Blake had been retained since 1980 as a landscape consultant to complete the plans. The Crosby Arboretum Foundation accomplished much in its first few years, but as Dorothy Crosby, wife of L. O. Crosby Jr., would remark, "Now all we need is an Arboretum!"[11]

Ed Blake was born in Pennsylvania but grew up in central Mississippi. His father owned a Christmas tree farm in Pocahontas, an unincorporated community near the state capital of Jackson, and as a child Blake walked the open pastures of evergreen trees dotted with Cherokee roses.[12] When his father allowed the land to regenerate back to nature, Blake saw this farm mature into a hardwood forest during his lifetime. Ed wrote of the correlation of Crosby Arboretum to his childhood farm in his journal in 1985: "The [Crosby Arboretum] Strawberry Farm is a return to my childhood."[13] Blake graduated from the MSU landscape architecture program in 1970, and after graduation he worked for a few years in landscape architecture firms in Kentucky and Kansas.

In 1977 Blake returned to his home state of Mississippi and MSU to teach in the Department of Landscape Architecture, and he observed: "I looked at my native land with new eyes. It's probably fair to say that I saw it for the first time."[14] McHarg's ideas were still taking root in the design profession and were novel concepts in the 1970s. In 1977 Blake attended a lecture by noted California landscape architect Garrett Eckbo, who told the audience that "an ecological approach to design will not occur until we believe we came out of the process."[15] In addition to his teaching appointment, Blake maintained a landscape consulting firm named after the solar home that he built and lived in, the Sun House.

Blake was contracted by the Crosby Foundation in 1980 to develop the arboretum's Master Plan, and within a year he initiated the first conceptual plan. Tom Bobbitt, then a student in the MSU landscape architecture program, continued to resolve Blake's ideas for the Crosby Arboretum plan in his final student project. Blake served as his faculty adviser, and together they worked with the input of the Crosby board. Board member Dr. George Switzer envisioned the arboretum to be a series of walking trails with niches carved out of the woods to feature individual native plants on the site. Bobbitt carried out this idea of plants on display, and his plan won a student award for design in 1982 from the Mississippi chapter of the American Society of Landscape Architects.[16]

As neither Blake nor the board had any experience in ecological design or in developing an arboretum's administrative structure, the Crosby Arboretum Foundation contracted with Andropogon Associates in 1982 to lead them through the Master Plan process. The addition of Andropogon brought a new level of energy to the project. Landscape architect and ecological designer Robert Poore later stated that it was from Andropogon that he and Blake first heard the term "processes and patterns," conveying the idea that a site's natural and cultural processes are expressed in its resulting vegetation signatures.[17] Understanding the site's processes and then incorporating the trajectory of the resulting vegetation patterns was the approach Andropogon would foster. On a similar note, Buckminster Fuller once stated, "I'm not trying to imitate nature, I'm trying to understand the principles she is using."[18]

Andropogon recommended that Crosby's botanists inform the designers about which plant communities would be appropriate for the arboretum's site. Andropogon would develop the conceptual design ideas, and Blake would resolve the working details of the Master Plan. Carol Franklin of Andropogon recalled that "over the years

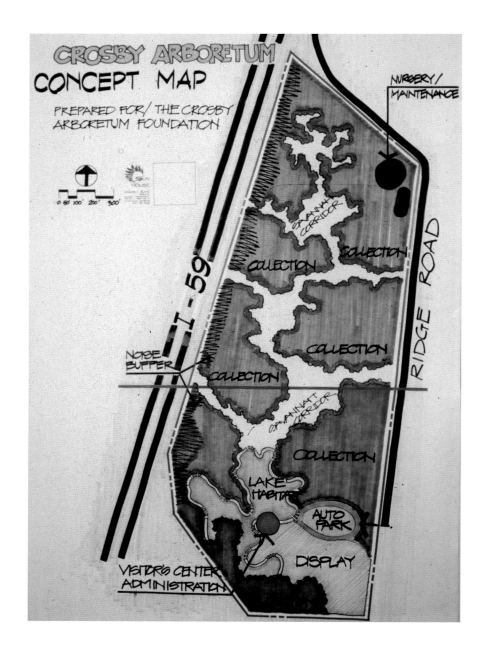

First Crosby Arboretum concept map drawn by Blake.

Photo courtesy of Crosby Arboretum

of our work with the Crosby we have perceived our role as creating a bridge between the scientific and artistic expertise available to the Arboretum," and that "Crosby was a significant leap for Andropogon as Leslie [Sauer] and I were teaching these [ecological] concepts in design, but nobody until the Crosby came along and said to do this thing on a massive scale."[19]

After a series of planning workshops, Andropogon developed a five-year plan to help the Crosby Arboretum take its first steps. The firm would assist the Crosby board in developing its statement of purpose and in outlining a strategic planning process. Knowing that the arboretum infrastructure would take time to develop, Andropogon proposed an open and participatory process, allowing arboretum visitors and members to become a part of early planning efforts. In this way, even though the landscape exhibits were not in place, the facility could begin to interpret the early research and management process. Andropogon proposed that Blake familiarize himself with the arboretum site by keeping a series of sketchbook journals. The designers saw Crosby as an evolving arboretum and wanted to document the changes that occurred throughout all phases of its development. They developed several tenets to guide the arboretum's growth:[20]

The ecological process of the site will determine all exhibit design and management. This was one of the most novel prescriptions, as most arboreta at the time contained a variety of plant collections, and not exhibits that incorporated natural process. Andropogon foresaw a change in the concept of botanic exhibits similarly to how zoos were changing their approaches to animal habitats. In the 1970s, zoos were mainly constructed as concrete enclosures in which animals were placed. Visitors learned little about the animals' natural habitats and often felt sympathetic toward the caged animals living in an artificial environment. The 1980s and 1990s saw revolutionary changes in zoo design as facilities across the country modified their animal enclosures to better reflect the species' natural environments.[21] Studies of zoo visitors found that they preferred seeing animals in enclosures that better reflected the animals' natural habitats.[22] Landscape architecture firms that were involved in designing zoo exhibits based on habitats included Jones and Jones (Seattle), Portico Group (Seattle), PGAV (St. Louis), and Design Consortium (New Orleans). The firms worked with animal biologists to provide for animal needs and safety and also to create conditions that allowed for the animals' social and recreational needs. Through habitat-based exhibits, visitors also came to a better understanding of the animals in their environmental contexts and their adaptations to unique conditions. Andropogon applied this concept to arboretum exhibits. At Crosby the firm proposed that plant community exhibits occur according to the site's environmental features for the entire facility. Andropogon wrote in Crosby's development guide that "the goal is not only to display the plant but the whole landscape in which it occurs, its companions, and the processes which have shaped it."[23]

The site will change over time. Rather than creating a planted landscape that simply matures, the Crosby Arboretum was to be dynamic in nature and management. This also ran counter to most arboretum management methods, which tend to leave an exhibit in a permanently fixed state. For example, when shrubs and trees expire in many garden exhibits, they are simply replaced with the same plant material, and the same lawns are mowed repeatedly in the same management patterns. The designers at Crosby instead proposed to allow the exhibits to pulse from both natural and man-caused disturbances, and to allow the plant species to shift over time. This defines the single major theme of the Crosby Arboretum that not only applied to the initial program efforts, but to the design of the arboretum as a whole: it is an evolutional landscape. Andropogon expounded the rationale for this idea:

- Succession and growth are concepts with which the forestry owners and biologists of the Crosby board of directors are already familiar.
- Evolution is a dynamic theme that encourages the visitor to come back again over time to observe the arboretum's change and growth. Allowing change invites visitors to become personally involved in the arboretum and to watch it grow.
- A dynamic site incorporates the life and goals of the arboretum's namesake, L. O. Crosby Jr., by "tying the past to the present and to the future." Evolution places the current use of the arboretum in the greater context of past uses and future trajectories.[24]

Thus the Crosby Arboretum organization and its exhibits would always be in a state of growth and change as the site matures and transitions to other forms. Similarly, the landscape exhibits such as the Woodland Exhibits would always be in various stages of vegetative evolution (also called succession or seral stages). In a forest system, even the death of an individual tree has its useful place by providing habitat and food for woodpeckers, owls, and numerous insect species. In this way, the Crosby Arboretum would allow for an appreciation of the entire cycle of life.

Because the arboretum site is mostly flat, the scale of any proposed visitor center or additions must be carefully considered as they would be very visible. This was true in the arboretum's early days when the entire 64 acres was an open understory with little shrub growth, allowing for easy visibility across the entire facility. The designers were concerned that any overbearing structures would dominate the view of the landscape. In "Outline for Developing the First-Year Program" (1983), they wrote: "Each built element must work to make the visitor more aware of the native landscape, which is the primary focus of the display, rather than draw attention to itself." They argued that the landscape is meant to be the exhibit. However, they acknowledge that structures can offer interesting ways of observing the landscape, "to be expressive of the storyline and to enable the visitor to see things in extraordinary ways, such as from high above or far below, compressed in time and space, heightened or dramatized."[25]

Growth and development of the arboretum should be slow and incremental. Rather than making a large commitment of resources at the beginning of its organization, which is often difficult to reverse, the arboretum would use exploratory development strategies that would result in minimal environmental impacts and resource allocations. This rationale for minimizing the upfront building and construction costs suited the early board well, as Crosby did not have a large established endowment of funds. A lack of resources often leads to innovative problem solving, which has proven itself repeatedly at the Crosby Arboretum.

A broad array of options will be considered before all major decisions are made. This tenet was related to the aforementioned lack of initial funds and was especially important in the early stages of phased site development. Having time to consider several options helps to prevent hasty mistakes that can easily occur when there are ample funds. Having patience when solving problems also allows the arboretum managers time to arrive at more creative, inspired solutions.

Every structural element, even if it performs a service function such as a parking area, shall be part of the exhibit and display. The entire site of the Interpretive Center was to be treated as a holistic educational unit. Constructed elements were to be derived from their surrounding environment and not detract from the landscape.

The exhibits at the Strawberry Farm will be modeled upon the natural areas, which shall remain undeveloped. As it was not possible to show all the possible plant communities in the region, especially those unsuited to the site or those requiring horticultural intervention, the exhibits were to be based only on potential habitats that would realistically thrive on the site. As stated in "Outline for Developing the First-Year Program," "it is at present neither possible nor desirable to attempt to represent all the plant communities found in the Pearl River Basin. The coastal and alluvial habitats would be extremely difficult to evoke, and their horticultural conditions problematic to establish. The acid, sandy environments, however, such as Talowah, Dead Tiger Savanna, Hammock, and the Pitcher Plant Meadows, all have parallel potential habitats on the Strawberry Farm site."[26] This approach obviated the need for horticultural changes that would be required if the designers decided to feature habitats that were not suited to the Interpretive Center. Many traditional garden practices change conditions to create the desired environment, instead of accepting the existing environment as the desired effect.

Habitat management will be greatest near the visitor center and major visitor nodes and transition toward unmanaged near the outer edges. Andropogon wrote: "There will be virtually no management at the wild edges. The wild and naturally succeeding landscape will serve as the context in which the arboretum and the exhibits are set, as well as provide a link to the landscapes beyond the site."[27] Thus the plantings and management of the exhibits would mostly occur by the pathways and use areas and less so toward the outer edges of the property.

With these guiding principles, Andropogon outlined the methods that would define the design and management strategies of the Crosby Arboretum. They pointed the way in which the Crosby Arboretum could fully devote itself to interpret the ecology of its surrounding landscape. These were radical new ideas in terms of arboretum design and environmental learning.

INFORMED FROM SCIENCE

In 1983, MSU's Sidney McDaniel and his graduate student Christopher Wells met with Ed Blake to discuss vegetation and fire patterns of the arboretum site.[28] At this meeting, the designer Blake first heard about the fine-scale vegetation responses on the property. McDaniel proposed an idea that, when it was finally realized, became a bold stroke in the layout of the arboretum. He recommended that the western half of the property no longer be burned but instead be allowed to grow into woodlands. When established, the woodlands would provide a visual and noise barrier to the interstate located on the western side of the site. This would also allow an ecological comparison of woodland species (which would soon emerge after the cessation of burning) with those of the open, burned savanna to the east. He suggested too that the arboretum feature its successional nature as "a living model of these complex ecological forces."[29] Finally, this model called for research and development to occur first in the savanna, which would allow the forest area time to mature.

McDaniel's ideas ultimately established the course of the Crosby Arboretum's layout, and in 1983 he began the first floristic surveys at the Interpretive Center. Just prior to this, the grid system was implemented for the entire 64-acre site with the installation of brass stakes. Blake presented McDaniel's suggestions to the arboretum's board in 1985. In his journal entry for that day, he outlined the rationale for organizing the facility into woodlands and savanna as McDaniel suggested.[30] First, the idea of exhibiting successional woodlands was something that had not been done before in an arboretum setting. Also, putting an initial emphasis on the development of the savanna exhibits as McDaniel had suggested would provide time to develop the Woodland Exhibits, as these would require many years to mature. Blake offered his knowledge of the long-term goals of other well-known parks, such as Central Park, to board members as comparisons. Educating the visiting public about savannas and fire management was also easily feasible as the grassland was already present. From a public garden perspective, the savanna offered summer flower color and visual diversity and interest. It gave visitors a chance to explore a wide diversity of plant species as a wealth of native orchids, bog plants, and wildflowers already flourished there. To take advantage of these existing opportunities would be the most fiscally prudent measure for a young organization struggling to articulate its mission, identify its constituents, and secure financial stability.

The task of the Crosby Arboretum was daunting: how to embody and condense key components of the Gulf Coast's Piney Woods region on a site of 64 acres. After a series of workshops in 1983 with Blake and Crosby's board of directors, Andropogon presented a schematic Master Plan to the board.[31] Early in the process, Andropogon mistakenly thought that the Crosby group was interested in displaying early Piney Woods cultural features, and the firm's first plan included rustic cabins, forestry implements, and other historical items. The board responded that it wanted to move forward in time and not backward, and rejected their initial plan. The board stated that the multiple historic and remnant features were too distracting on such a small site and that they were more interested in plant habitats than inhabitations. Some board members argued that the arboretum should just be a walk in the woods; in any case, it was an easy fix to remove the cultural features from the Master Plan.[32] These initial studies did, however, establish some important planning decisions that would persist in the final form of the Master Plan, including the location of the Piney Woods Lake and the layout of the main circulation elements.

To conceptualize how the exhibits were going to be organized in the plan, Ed Blake simply added the missing component—people—to Sidney McDaniel's graph of plant community interactions. Blake had referred to these three elements—fire, water, and people—as the dominant interacting forces within the Piney Woods landscape, both historically and today. At Crosby, fire would be represented in the savanna, which is maintained by burning; water would be displayed in the constructed wetlands and in the moisture levels of the soil; and people through site management: the pathways, the construction of buildings, art exhibits, and other visitor needs. Much of the Master Plan's efforts would center on providing for people to encounter—and engage with—

the landscape. The fluidity and interaction between these three forces would shape Crosby's exhibits into an evolving structure. This triad of fire, water, and people as the arboretum's focus would convey the point that humans are an intrinsic part of nature and not separate. These three forces have direct impacts on one another as the resulting landscape patterns emerge.

The overall complexity of the forms of the Master Plan replicates the complexity of the subtle moisture patterns of the property. Blake was strongly influenced by the work of landscape architect John Simonds, who once wrote that "a final form must be derived from a planned experience rather than the experience from the preconceived form."[33] Similarly, Blake believed that form should be an organic expression of the experience.

The Master Plan would incorporate the prior agricultural and forestry disturbances that were still evident. The old farm ditches, roads, and fire breaks were present on the grounds, now with trees and shrubs growing out of them. Most conservation organizations would readily erase these cultural scars of the past by filling in the ditches and removing the roads, but instead these remnants were viewed at Crosby signs of nature healing itself and adapting to human interventions—as nature has always done. Some forty years after the end of the Strawberry Farm, pond cypress and water oak trees were growing from the edges of old ditches, and pines were emerging from the beds of previous farm roads. This insight of nature adapting to and healing the human-induced landscape led Blake to adopt the Thomas Berry concept of the universe becoming conscious of itself.[34] Thomas Berry was a priest, eco-theologian, and author of numerous books concerning the deep spirituality of earth systems. Berry and his coauthor Brian Swimme (a mathematical cosmologist) describe the universe as a story that can be read, which inspired Blake to view the Crosby Arboretum as a microcosm of natural process that reflects a larger universal story.

The Crosby Arboretum's Master Plan was viewed as just another layer of intervention to the landscape, one that is laid upon the previous human and natural events through deep time. The trails, ponds, and buildings are but a thin veneer on top of the arboretum's deeper stratums of sand and silt. Dan Earle, professor emeritus of landscape architecture at Louisiana State University, often brought classes to Crosby. He observed, "I think of Crosby on a geological scale and land that has an evolution and a story to tell—a story that is continuing with new layers laid down by real people. Everyone knows about the Pavilion which is great, but it sometimes overwhelms the real story. It had a geological base, Native Americans influenced it (probably by fire), the Crosby's did with lumber and strawberries, and finally the Arboretum. But each left its mark that is still there."[35] Indeed, in the early arboretum years it was rather easy to "read the landscape" in terms of the forest structure. One could readily see the even-aged canopy pines that were planted in the 1940s, with a clear line of emerging understory forest that occurred from the cessation of burning in the 1980s, and finally the lower layer of plants that were introduced in the late 1980s and 1990s. Today, thirty years after its beginnings, the forest structure of the Interpretive Center is blurred together and merges the past and present.

The arboretum's Master Plan allowed for natural disturbances, and subsequent healings, to fully occur on the site. The plan acknowledged that over time, hurricanes and tornadoes would devastate forest canopies; nearby creeks and rivers would flood regularly; and extended droughts were certain to happen. Weather patterns and even the climate itself would shift and change. Each of these disruptions would alter the trajectories of the forest and bring change. Here, at Crosby, this propensity for change would be embraced, not lamented; efforts would focus on interpreting these natural changes to the visiting public as the arboretum's main narrative. Matthew Potteiger and Jamie Purinton discuss this issue in their book *Landscape Narratives* (1998), noting that the "Crosby Arboretum uses the indeterminancy of ecological processes to create an open narrative which develops over time."[36] The never-ending story of events and time, and how nature responds to events, is captured in the square-eye lens of the arboretum's interlocking grid systems. Documenting the biological changes that occur in the grids gives a permanent reference in which to mark change through time.

Dr. McDaniel and Chris Wells documented all plant species and locations for each grid cell in the years of 1982 and 1987, with the idea that vegetation studies would be conducted in five-year intervals. Although grant money was not secured to sample the vegetation regularly, the staff did record successional changes (the growth of savanna to forest exhibits) on the site by photographing certain grid corners over a number of

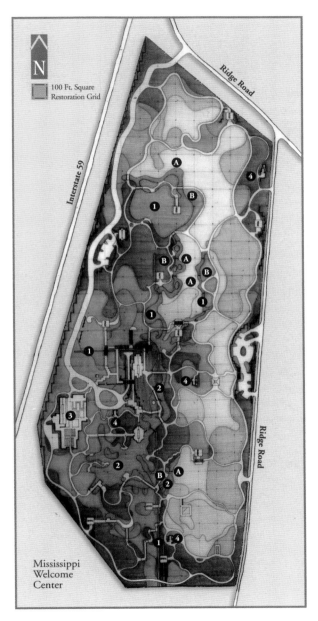

This map shows the moisture patterns of the Interpretive Center site for the Woodland, Savanna, and Wetland exhibits, and directed the final Master Plan.

Photo courtesy of Crosby Arboretum

years. Arboretum staff made strides to document every plant that was installed on the property for both species type and the grid location planted. This site information, coupled with successional vegetation research for the Gulf Coast, would aid biologists in reconstructing vegetation changes at the arboretum over time.

Although the ideas of water, forest, and savanna were already being developed by 1984 after approval of the first concept plan, the Master Plan would continue to be fine-tuned in form and function for another decade. Each passing year brought a new level of refinement to the Crosby plan, until it was completed and approved by the board in 1994. Because of its subtle complexities, the plan took fourteen years to study and resolve with the understanding that as an evolving and dynamic arboretum, the facility would also change through time. Lynn Gammill recalled in 2011 that "Ed Blake was a unique individual and had so many dimensions to his personality. I used to tease him, you know, haste was not one of his qualities. You can look at the early board meeting minutes and it says Ed will have Master Plan completed in four years. Thank goodness he waited because we learned more every year about what we wanted to do."[37] It was conceived that changes to the plan would continue to occur over time with the same aspirations and ideals as originally envisioned, but perhaps in a more sophisticated fashion as new ideas in biology, ecology, and materials emerged.

THE EXHIBITS

> This is a subtle landscape and will require subtly designed interventions.
> —Andropogon Associates, "Outline for Developing the First-Year Program of the Crosby Arboretum," 1983

Genius loci and sense of place became important qualities guiding my perception of landscape's architecture. Pursuing these ideas led me to thirteen years of work that quietly changed my life. At the Crosby Arboretum, in Picayune, Mississippi, I listened for and found my voice. During my tenure at Crosby, I was privileged to collaborate with many gifted people. Each one worked with us to establish the Arboretum's conceptual foundation. I lived with Pinecote's 64 acres for a decade and came to know its expressive qualities intimately. I gained insights of how landscapes are perceived from all who interacted

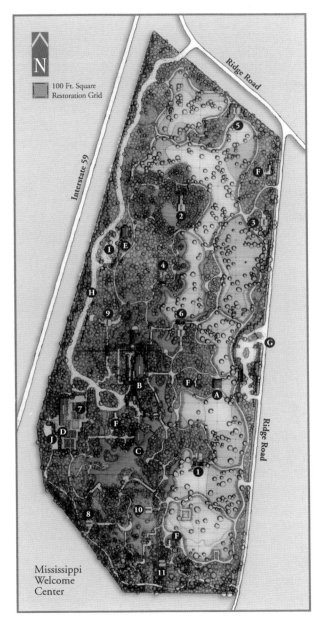

MASTER PLAN

Savanna

Freshwater Wetland

Woodland

Buildings

Ⓐ Switzer Orientation Center

Ⓑ Visitor's Center

Ⓒ Pinecote Pavilion

Ⓓ Restoration Center

Ⓔ Administrative Center

Ⓕ Rest Rooms

Circulation

Ⓖ Visitor's Entrance and Parking

Ⓗ Service Road

Ⓘ Business Office Parking

Ⓙ Staff and Volunteer Parking

Path Journeys through Landscape Exhibits

Landscape Interpretive Stations

❶ Pitcher Plant Bog

❷ Gum Pond

❸ Longleaf Pine

❹ Woodland

❺ Savanna

❻ Savanna-Woodland Transition

❼ Plant Propagation

❽ Woodland Succession

❾ Bay Gall

❿ Shrub Bog

⓫ Piney Woods

The 1994 Master Plan of the Crosby Arboretum.

Photo courtesy of Crosby Arboretum

with this place. I worked to write more succinctly and found words to be a powerful way of seeing. I began to see the land as culture-nature signatures of time and place. I crafted stories to interpret the Arboretum for our visitors. They explored the poetics of form.

—Edward L. Blake Jr., Landscape Studio website, 2010

Ed Blake wrote in 2006 that the arboretum's exhibits are a "manifestation of the phenomena."[38] In other words, what one sees and experiences in one of the exhibits is the direct result of the physical and environmental forces that shaped its resulting vegetative structure. As can be inferred from Dr. McDaniel's graph, pitcher plants are evidence of wet acidic soils and frequent disturbance by fire or mowing; beech forests result from the lack of fire or storms and medium-moisture soils; and water lilies are tied to deeper, permanent water bodies. The unique factors of a site result from its combination of soils, climate, hydrology, plant and soil seed bank, animal impacts, and human and natural disturbance. These items give rise to the forms and aesthetics of a place. Blake summarized this in 2004: "form expressive of structure, structural form expressive of phenomena, structural integrity expressive of fitness, fitness expressive of beauty, health and well-being."[39] At Crosby, the land is the exhibit, the land is the story, and the land's form reveals what happened in its creation.

The job of the designer, then, is to weave a human experience through the already storied environment and to clarify the existing elements that perhaps obscure the exhibit's forms and shapes. This may be done by what Blake called "landscape editing," or the pruning and removing of vegetative elements that block a landscape's aesthetic. He described this process in his 2003 notebook, writing that one can "add by taking away," and called the existing site a "landscape's architecture"—or the existing physical vegetation or topography constituting its structural elements.[40] By using the principles and elements of design, the designer reveals and augments the beauty and integrity of the inherent landscape, in whatever form that may take.

Blake was encouraged by Andropogon Associates to create an immersive experience for the trails of Crosby Arboretum. To accomplish this, he was inspired by the work of the Mississippi Gulf Coast artist Walter Anderson. Living in the coastal community of Ocean Springs, Mississippi, in the early twentieth century, Anderson would row his little wooden boat into the Mississippi Sound to a nearby barrier island. Here he would live freely out in nature for days as he wished: painting, writing, and dancing.[41] Anderson painted vibrant watercolors that captured the colors and scenes of the Mississippi Gulf Coast. More important, in shamanlike fashion, he captured the spirit or *genius loci* in his art. Art critic Patti Carr Black called Anderson "the most outstanding artist the South has produced."[42]

Like Anderson, Blake had a childlike wonder of nature, marveling over the com-

Early sketch by Blake showing the walk through the Gum Pond Exhibit at Crosby Arboretum, 1983.

Sketch courtesy of Crosby Arboretum

mon sights and sounds of the landscape that most people took for granted. Following Anderson's lead, he sought to experience the arboretum site fully for what it had to offer. Blake spent long days and nights on the site, peering between grass blades and into ditches, always asking himself and others who might know, "Why is this happening here?" He would rise early in the morning to photograph the subtle yet ever-changing light qualities of the landscape. In 1983, Blake wrote, "I spent last summer in search of the 'Zen essence' or 'genius' of the Arboretum and its environs. I filled three notebooks recording my direct field observations of plant responses to their coastal plain environments."[43] The content of his numerous sketchbooks ranged from drawings and notes about plant species growing along the ditches to poetic observations of clouds and light in the Mississippi sky. Blake used his notebooks to address questions that he was trying to solve concerning the arboretum exhibits. He was a voracious reader and often had eight to ten volumes stacked near his reading chair, ranging from classics in philosophy to landscape architecture works. Key passages in his books were underlined and heavily annotated, always making analogies and justifications for his projects at hand.

To Blake, experiencing the pathways of the arboretum would provide today's public with brief glimpses of their ancestral landscape. He saw this as increasingly important at a time when Mississippi's rural landscapes were changing into sprawling residential and commercial developments. Blake did not even recognize the need for interpreting this landscape to visitors through signage or brochures until he was pressured to do so by the visiting public. To him, the sights, sounds, and smells of the arboretum's landscape were an exhilarating—and personal—experience of changes in light, life, and substance that needed no structured explanation.

The work of noted landscape architect Lawrence Halprin was another motivating force upon Blake's design psyche. He wrote in 2009 that "Halprin's work and writings have affected me greatly. His book RSVP Cycles changed the way I began to conceptualize my work. The resulting idea of scoring movement sequences to affect sensual experience of place was the basis of my work at Crosby Arboretum."[44] Halprin's wife Anne was a dancer, and her choreographed movements shaped how Halprin saw users of his plazas and parks as they moved through the landscape. In the design of Crosby,

Blake's locations of pathways and seating areas provided a rhythm that choreographed how visitors experienced the site.

But to Blake, above all else, nothing should distract the visitor from the passive immersion of studying light patterns and plant textures, and the unfolding discoveries along the pathways. Andropogon's Leslie Sauer conceived of the pathways as "journeys" or an adventure to be undertaken.[45] The arboretum's journeys were programmed as a sort of Deep South interpretation of a Chinese scholar's garden, a place that provides meditative environments instead of more active programming. The Crosby Arboretum's journeys were designed for two distinct purposes: first, for education about the local environment, and second, for contemplation.[46] In the early 1980s there were natural places along the Gulf Coast, but few provided interpretation of the natural environment. At the Crosby Arboretum, the land was the exhibit and the pathways were the sequences that helped reveal how the land expresses itself.

Bob Grese, director of the Matthaei Botanical Gardens and Nichols Arboretum at the University of Michigan, noted, "I loved the notion of the paths through the [Crosby] Arboretum being termed 'pathway journeys.' It emphasizes the design of paths as being intentionally experiential—not just a route from A to B."[47] For the layout of pathways, Andropogon's Carol Franklin passed along to Blake a short garden narrative by the American designer Russel Wright, the noted mid-twentieth-century designer of furnishings, dinnerware, and fabrics for the modern home environment.[48] Wright tucked his home and studio into an old abandoned quarry in Garrison, New York, and ultimately created a 75-acre natural "garden," complete with pathways to many of the existing features and views. Wright named the place Manitoga and wrote four simple rules for planning paths:

1. Follow the natural contour of the land. Unless you are trying to develop an *allée,* avoid straight lines. Make paths that always curve.
2. If possible, make it unnecessary to retrace your steps on a path; that is, make it complete a contour.
3. Plan it to show off the most interesting features of your land. Have it pass through a bed of ferns; turn around a knoll or a rock formation.

4. Vistas should be cut very slowly. Do not make the usual crude mistake of a panoramic vista by cutting down everything in front of the viewer. It should be framed with large trees, and have many trees between the viewer and the vista to create more depth and a subtle, natural effect.[49]

Blake followed each of these rules religiously in planning the arboretum's pathways. His paths arc gracefully throughout the facility and offer few straight lines, except near the central core of buildings. Few paths result in dead ends, and they mostly link into other journeys. The pathways were planned to bring visitors to unique features such as a leaning tree, an unusual vine, or a witch's broom (a deformity in a tree or shrub that causes a dense mass of shoots). Blake made the most of natural gateways, or transitions along the pathways. He often wove paths between two trees to create a framing device for the view ahead.

Of utmost importance to Blake in designing Crosby's pathways was providing the visitor with direct contact to the environments, so as to not "lose the real thing."[50] There would be no elevated boardwalks, but simple curving paths of compacted soil where natural elements are up close and all around. Similar to how Walter Anderson experienced his landscapes, Blake could be in the midst of the most common pine woodland and approach it with fresh eyes. He wrote that "the smell of a thunder shower, the sight of a bog orchid, the soft textured feel of club moss, the taste of a blueberry and the sound of the wind through the crowns of the longleaf pine—all these human experiences are part of that synthesis."[51]

Jory Johnson, commenting on the Crosby Arboretum's landscape as a contemporary story, wrote in his 1991 book *Modern Landscape Architecture:* "The Crosby Arboretum, for instance, structures our experience with stage directions—both written, in the Arboretum's interpretive literature; and physical, in the slow twists and turns of the path system. Like all modern narratives, the Crosby Arboretum is an attempt to communicate deep human meaning without abstruse symbols or prior knowledge."[52] In *Landscape Narratives,* Potteiger also takes this meaning at Crosby further into time, stating that "the site is in the process of becoming a complex, braided, and evolving narrative of ecological time."[53]

Interpretation was perceived to best be handled at Crosby through the use of visitor films or learning centers dispersed throughout the facility. Interpretive media could compress the variations that would occur through time. Ultimately, traditional signage systems, including pathway signs, were needed to explain each exhibit's nuances to the general public. While Blake initially resisted interpretive signage, eventually this educational feature was added along Crosby's pathways.

As the Master Plan was being developed by Blake and Andropogon Associates, the board felt a compelling need to have some first trail or feature in place. Carol Franklin credited partners Colin Franklin and Leslie Sauer for much of the concept and design of this initial trail.[54] Andropogon developed the conceptual plan for the path, and Hartley Fairchild, a landscape architect from nearby Hattiesburg, assisted on the pathway layout. In 1984, a short introductory trail loop was established in the region of the Pitcher Plant Bog Exhibit at the extreme southern end of the Interpretive Center. Designers made use of an existing parking lot located across the road at a local Veterans of Foreign War hall and provided for a short 400-foot walking trail.[55] The trail provided an important, brief glimpse of what the arboretum would ultimately become and allowed its designers to test their ideas on the first visiting groups.

This first interpretive trail allowed the local community to get a glimpse of the new arboretum. A few early visitors were bewildered that a place would spend money to interpret meadows and woodlands right in the middle of existing meadows and woodlands. But the early founders anticipated the future as Picayune grew in population: this 64-acre native plant arboretum would become a remnant green space in the midst of an urban sea of homes and commercial businesses. As shown by several well-known urban parks, including Central Park in New York and Golden Gate State Park in San Francisco, open land preserved adjacent to developing urban centers would eventually become an invaluable community asset. Just a decade after the Crosby was established, a big-box retail store was constructed about a mile from its front gates. In a classic case of urban sprawl, numerous businesses leapfrogged from Picayune's retail epicenter and populated areas adjacent to the arboretum, providing a jarring contrast and adding another layer of complexity to the arboretum's narrative. As the nearby community becomes more urbanized, the Crosby Arboretum becomes a touchstone for its population to interact with the native landscape.

The work on the Master Plan progressed, and the decision was made to construct a two-acre lake exhibit and pavilion. Ed Blake wrote about this phase of the project: "As a major display feature at the Strawberry Farm, the Piney Woods Lake will be the central focus from which further display enrichment will spread. . . . As most of the introduced aquatic plants will be fast-growing herbaceous ones, a relatively mature-looking display can be achieved in a short time period."[56] He had some initial thoughts about providing a shelter and that it should "act as a compass itself by fitting into the overall site grid."[57] After being drenched during one of his early group tours, he stated, "You can't learn by slogging in the rain."[58] The board agreed with Blake on the need for a shelter that would also serve as a place for the first educational programs. Crosby family members donated the initial funding for the building, and board members began to search for a suitable architect.

4

THE ARCHITECTURE OF FAY JONES

Organic architecture has a central generating idea; as in most organisms
every part and every piece has a relationship. Each should benefit the
other; there should be a family of form, and pattern. You should feel the
relationship to the parts and to the whole.

—E. Fay Jones, 1992

Euine Fay Jones was always interested in building. As a high school student in Pine Bluff, Arkansas, he once saw a short film on the Johnson Wax building in Racine, Wisconsin. The architect of the building was Frank Lloyd Wright, and
this brief glimpse of a futuristic building inspired Fay to make his career as an architect. Jones enrolled at the University of Arkansas, but since the school did not offer
architecture classes at that time, he enrolled in engineering. Jones's education was
interrupted by World War II when he served as a pilot in the Pacific theater. Upon
his return home, he found that the University of Arkansas had initiated an architecture department under the direction of John Williams, an Arkansas native who advocated for Prairie School principles of regional architecture. Jones enrolled and studied
Wright's works, admiring the "rightness of Wright's style" and his works that strove to
unite the site and architecture into an organic whole.[1] After meeting Wright in 1949,
Jones accepted his offer to intern one summer at Taliesin East in Wisconsin. Completing his summer internship in 1954, Jones returned to the University of Arkansas to
teach in the architecture department, where he later served as department chair and
then dean. While working at the university, Jones began a small architecture practice in the 1950s, which he maintained until his retirement from both in 1988. Maurice Jennings, one of Jones's students, joined his practice in 1973 and later became his

partner. Jennings was involved in many of the design and construction details for Crosby Arboretum's pavilion.

Robert Ivy, executive director of the American Institute of Architects, described Fay Jones as one of Frank Lloyd Wright's gifted students. Similar to Wright, Jones had an affinity for using local building materials in his structures and maintained that the building and its constructions should have only slight impacts on the site. Whereas Wright was from the Midwest, Jones was from the South and therefore had a distinct interest in southern vernacular architecture. Jones's philosophy of how structures should fit within nature would guide his work, and he stated that architecture is but an instrument upon which nuances of nature can play.[2]

In 1983, the Crosby board of directors, having decided to construct a building in which to hold programs, placed a call for project proposals among Mississippi ar-

Fay Jones at the location for the future Pinecote Pavilion with building model, 1984.

chitects. At this same time, Ed Blake had heard from a friend about a new chapel in
Eureka Springs, Arkansas. The building was Thorncrown Chapel, designed by Fay
Jones, and Blake made a special trip to see it. Blake met with Jones at Thorncrown and
brought back photos of the structure to show the Crosby board. Thorncrown Chapel
was Fay Jones's masterpiece. Called "a prayer from the human heart," Thorncrown has
since been cited as one of the ten best buildings of the twentieth century.[3]

The Crosby board extended Jones an invitation to design a pavilion where the arboretum could hold events. Jones would turn down other offers of work in order to
complete the Crosby Arboretum pavilion, noting, "I'm impressed with both the site
and the people involved. Their sensitivity to the landscape and their attempts to instill
these ideals in future generations is indeed a noble goal."[4]

After a series of exploratory sketches, Jones presented his ideas to the board, and
they were enraptured with the design for the pavilion. One of the few concerns came

from the board president, who was worried that the large roof would appear too heavy and dark inside. Jones responded by peeling back the layers of the roof edges in the design, exposing the supports to the sky. Writer and landscape architect Lake Douglas later described this latticed roof edge as the "poetics of revealed construction."[5] Jones thought of the deconstructed roof as a way to "allow plants to intermingle with the buildings and further strengthen the symbiosis of the built and natural environments."[6] Partner Jennings added, "What makes the pavilion tingle is the roofline: light and lacelike. It's the feathering of the edges just like the pine trees. This led to the design which came very quickly."[7] Jones noted, "Usually you're covering a roof out to the edge. But the roof at Pinecote comes up just so far, and then there are half as many shingles and a certain rhythm with the boards, and its changing stages. It kind of dissolves." As Gareth Fenley noted, "Like the pine straw and pine limbs, they progressively thin out from something that's close and dense to something open and fragile."[8]

Jones called the pavilion design an "abstract forest," alluding to the form-giving principles embodied in the structure.[9] Robert Ivy wrote of the open-air structure, "The line between 'out' and 'in' is blurred; the feeling is of finding shelter within the out-of-doors."[10] In selecting colors, Jones employed Wright's dictum to "go to the woods and fields for color schemes."[11] The gray stain used on the pavilion's wooded supports echos the muted appearance of pine and hardwood trees, while the bright orange paint on metal pieces reflects the ocher hues of pine bark and the winter color of bluestem grass. Another way in which the pavilion reflects its surroundings can be seen in the cross bracing of the pavilion's supports, which match the angle of the surrounding slash pine branches emerging from their trunks. Multiple posts arising from the tile floor resemble the clustering of pine trunks in a forest, and the notched pavilion posts emulate blocky pine bark.

The pavilion was originally conceived to be one part of several structures connected to a visitor's center and an office building, and some of the early renderings show this relationship. However, the board was concerned that the visitor's center and office buildings were too close to the pavilion and would detract from its contemplative quality. Subsequent designs placed the structures out of sight of what would be christened the Pinecote Pavilion.

Pinecote Pavilion shown in its surrounding context.

Photo by Ed Blake Jr., courtesy of Marilyn Blake

Crosby forestry resources were invaluable in the construction of the pavilion. Timber crews built the service road for the construction equipment and cleared the site. The Crosby family allowed the architect to select his own timber for the pavilion from a local woodlot. Jennings recalled: "Fay and I came down to pick the trees from Crosby lands, which was then treated and kiln-dried at the Crosby's mill. Unfortunately by the time we came to claim the wood someone else took the wood we had selected, so we had to go out and pick them out all over again."[12]

Pinecote Pavilion was completed and dedicated on November 23, 1986. It received numerous awards from a variety of architectural societies, including a 1990 Honor Award from the American Institute of Architects (AIA). This award secured for Jones the AIA's most coveted prize, the Gold Medal, of which he was the forty-eighth recipient.

The 4,000-square-foot pavilion is cathedral-like in form, echoing the surrounding tall pine trees. Just after completing the design, Jones wrote, "I think there is an uplifting, poetic quality to the pavilion . . . which invites meditation and contemplation," and that the skylight opens light into the darkest part of the building to enhance the play of light below, as well as to "establish a mood of participation with nature."[13] The predominant building material was wood, which Jones felt appropriate to a facility featuring plants, as well as that the "building will appear to have come out of the region, rather than looking as though it was imported from elsewhere."[14] Jones sensitively worked in his own observations of the pine forest. As he noted about its origins from nature, "Lots of little pieces were used, so that it blends in with the general grain, texture, and flow of the trees and leaves."[15]

I first met Fay Jones in 1991 under the sheltering roof of Pinecote Pavilion and asked him how he had organized the building. He wordlessly traced his foot along the edge of the wooden slats that are geometrically gridded into the tiled floor. He only said, "It all starts from the foundation." Here he implied that the organization began where the posts originated from the wooden grid corners. This framework supports and organizes the rest of the building.

As the pavilion would have no walls, thus no heating or cooling devices, Jones cleverly positioned the structure for maximum effect from the local climate. The length of the building extends north to south, and the broad, sheltering roof shades the majority of the floor space during hot summer days. In winter, however, with the sun at a much lower angle in the sky, more of the warming rays reach farther into the interior of the pavilion to heat the brick tiles. Conversely, as heat rises to the pavilion roof in summer, the raised glass of the center skylight vents the heat outside. Even the shape of the surrounding Piney Woods Lake was considered in the climactic effects. The length of the pond is laid in a south-southwesterly direction from the pavilion. The Gulf Coast summer breezes mostly come from this direction, which allows the wind to slightly cool the air before it enters the pavilion.

A striking aspect of the pavilion is its play of light—night or day. Jones commented that "the most potent force in architecture is how you handle light" and that the daylight allows a filtered light through the pavilion edges and skylight, whereas at night "it really delineates the openness of the roof."[16]

Pinecote Pavilion is a gathering place. This simple, open building marks a place to be used for many activities. It is a starting point for nature walks, for talks and discussions about important things in the environment and the natural world, a place for exhibits and artistic performance, and a setting for social gatherings.

Architecturally, Pinecote is a symmetrical shed, resting on a base of earth-toned brick, surrounded by earth, water, and trees. The brick pattern expresses the basic building module—the composition and arrangement of all the vertical columns. The all-wood structure is built of an indigenous material, native pine, and is fastened together with nails, dowels, and metal connectors. There is complete exposure of every construction element, all visible from within and without. Every framing member, every beam, brace and connection is absolutely necessary to achieve structural stability.

The building is ordered by a geometric theme—the step-edge pattern that defines the outline of the base and the roof's outer edges. Many smaller elements, for lighting and display, are shaped and detailed to reflect and reinforce the characteristic geometry—to build a strong relationship of each part to the whole and to achieve an organic unity.

As the vertical supports rise from the brick pavement, there is a spreading-out of structural members and a progressive thinning-out of the roof decking toward the edges of the hovering roof. There is a transition in the sheltering overhead arrangement, accented by a central ridge skylight, from close and dense to open and fragile. This is analogous to the organic unfolding, or blossoming, of so many forms of botanical growth. The imbricated pattern of the wood shingles also emulate and recall many of nature's surfaces—the bark of trees and the wings of birds. All wood is stained and metal painted in colors that will harmonize with the earth and the plants.

Nothing has been added to the structure as mere decoration. Ornamentation, or decorative enrichment, will come from the ever-changing patterns of light and shadows that will play on the closely-shaped structural elements as the sun and moon move across the sky. Time of day and seasonal changes will modify the shadows that frame the light and will keep the spaces in and around Pinecote vital and alive, continuously enhancing the poetics of revealed construction.

—E. Fay Jones, 1986

A GROWING OUTWARD

There is a fundamental understanding of landscape ecology expressed in the wood and metal of Pinecote Pavilion. Yet the structure is not a direct imitation of nature. Jones would clarify this by stating that "organic does not mean having the building look like a bush. It is the central generator."[17] Fay stated that "the effect of the Pavilion would not be one of the building, nor of the landscape, it would be one of something between, it would be of a higher realm."[18]

Just as Andropogon Associates would strongly influence Ed Blake's thoughts on ecological design, Fay Jones's thoughts and expression in Pinecote Pavilion would eventually radiate throughout the arboretum site. For Blake, the concept of the pavilion was metaphor for life spreading outward from its origins, or dissolving outward. This was perhaps best expressed in the layout of the Pond Journey, where Jones's design for the bridges and weirs appear as extensions of the pavilion. Blake would weave these architectural motifs throughout the plan for Crosby's sixty-four acres, later stating that this holistic approach to the arboretum's design was "the most important thing that I have accomplished at the Crosby Arboretum."[19]

The Interpretive Center became a study in proportion, with the 100-foot grid pattern extending out from the pavilion's floor and organizing the whole facility. Jones used the time-honored proportions of the Golden Ratio in much of the design of Pinecote Pavilion. The Golden Ratio uses an irrational constant number (1.618 . . .) for length-to-width proportions.[20] Since the time of the Greeks, artists, mathematicians, and architects have found this geometric number ratio to be aesthetically pleasing. Utilizing this architectural motif in the Master Plan, Blake also conceived of the proportion of the arboretum's woodlands to open savanna (2/3 woodland, 1/3 savanna).

Jones wrote that the pavilion would "play a strong part in the whole organic relationship idea—trying to have everything all of a piece, looking like it stemmed from a single source."[21] This idea of "each part to the whole" was also espoused by Jones's mentor Frank Lloyd Wright, who wrote that "the part is to the whole as the whole is to the part."[22] To achieve the intentional holistic effect in his houses, Jones designed nearly all elements in the residence from the dishes to lights to furnishings, in similar

The orientation of the Emergent Cove bridge centers on Pinecote Pavilion.

fashion to Wright. Jones also designed a number of buildings and site amenities for the Crosby Arboretum, but most were never constructed due to construction costs.

These other structural designs include the Switzer Pavilion (an orientation center to be located near the visitors' parking entry); the Visitors Center (an education center); a small separate office grouping known as the Administration Center; and the Restoration Center (maintenance facility). Jones developed the conceptual renderings for these buildings but not the construction details. Several of his smaller-scaled designs were built and installed at the arboretum, including its front entry gates and wall, a water fountain (with a Mesoamerican theme), a pond weir, an outdoor restroom, an artesian well pumphouse, information kiosks, a lectern, bridges, benches, and two of the most elegant copper-topped trashcans ever conceived. Other unconstructed items include designs for the pathway lighting, pathway signage, bollards, and a boot scraper. These elements, while smaller in scale than proposed structures,

The Slough weir and nearby bridge, 2006.

show Jones's concern for the entire design experience and his capacity to treat even the smallest element—such as a lectern or a pond weir—with as much attention as a building.

Applying principles from Jones and Wright, Blake structured the Crosby Master Plan as an entity with organic unity. He wrote in the Master Plan narrative that "each component contributes to the purpose, health, and integrity of the whole and in doing so forges new relationships between culture and nature."[23]

There were other influences of Jones that would radiate out into the landscape of the arboretum. Jones freely utilized ideas from the historic buildings that he admired and noted that "history can serve as a 'generator of ideas,' not merely a source for copyists."[24] At his Gold Medal acceptance speech, he stated, "Any bridges to the future must connect with the past."[25] Blake likewise sought design solutions from the great landscape works. The peripheral walk around the Savanna Journey strongly echoes the Great Meadow walk at New York's Central Park. The Pond Journey sets the stage for Pinecote Pavilion to be viewed from various points along the pond—essentially a modern interpretation of the pavilion at Kinkakuji, the Golden Pavilion at Kyoto, Japan. Jones established a strong mathematical structure and order to his building footprints.[26] Blake espoused this design element by using the site grid as an ordering device for the location of buildings and pathways. These influences from other works were viewed as precedents or inspirations for solving a particular design problem.

Jones selected the name "Pinecote" for the pavilion at Crosby. Broken into its simplest terms, "pine-cote" translates as "pine-house." "Cote," of Old English origin, means "shelter" or "coop." Blake extended the term Pinecote to describe the whole of the arboretum's grounds. Blake saw the role of architecture at the arboretum as representing some permanent feature in the landscape. Much of the rest of nature, such as grasses and wildflowers coming in and out of bloom, was viewed as temporal. Blake wrote that he saw structures as the site's stability, "like a river gauge" allowing the processes of nature to wash over.[27] Blake understood and appreciated nature's fluidity, by which forms come into being and disappear, and he saw this phenomenon in very human terms. As visitors to Angkor Wat and Mayan temples experience, there is a poignant tension to be felt in the presence of finely crafted architectural expressions that nature ultimately swallows.

5

DESIGN AND CONSTRUCTION
OF THE PINEY WOODS LAKE

What triggered all this again on Sunday was seeing the black water
reflections of the slough crossing just north of the weir. Water, bridge and
wax myrtle were one. At the cypress head landing water, pavilion, and
cypress were one, each more vivid because of its other.
                                        —Ed Blake to Fay Jones, 2003

From discussions with other garden directors, the arboretum staff realized that Pinecote needed a major attraction beyond the plant community concept, and they determined that feature would relate to water. Blake summarized the need for an aquatic exhibit: "Utilizing the magic that water extracts from the human psyche, we hope to heighten the experience of visiting the Arboretum."[1] Carol Franklin concurred with the need for a pond to entice visitors, later saying that "you cannot sell an aquarium with brown fish in it, no matter how beautifully designed."[2] Blake reasoned that as Pinecote already had a high water table, the addition of a pond would only serve to dramatize the effect of water on plants.[3] A pond would offer visitors a chance to see the third major ecosystem component and to complete the conceptual triad of fire, water, and people. A pond was a major departure for the site; examples of ponds in the region were sought out for research, but south Mississippi soils did not offer many natural ponds except in the alluvial floodplains of rivers, where oxbow lakes abound.

The arboretum site did not have a stream or creek or oxbow lake, so the designers opted to conceptualize another naturally occurring water body: a beaver pond. Mississippi has a wealth of stream channels that once teemed with beavers. Examples of these impounded water bodies were evident in the region and became rich models for

The Piney Woods Lake
Exhibit, 2006

Photo by Ed Blake Jr., courtesy of Marilyn Blake

study. Blake included such a pond among his early programming ideas for the arboretum, noting that it should be "1–2 acres in size and should have a lot of water plant diversity."[4]

Blake reasoned that the proposed pond and water exhibits would make the existing wetlands more apparent and offer more opportunities for wildlife habitat. A study from 1983 mapping the wetland configurations of the arboretum site would directly inspire the wetland locations of the Master Plan. The pond depression banked up next to a dense grove of pine trees, an area in the heart of the site that architect Jones identified as the most suitable location for the pavilion. Blake and Andropogon staff formed the shape of the pond by staking the perimeter of the contours of the existing wetland depression. Carol Franklin explained, "If, indeed, there had been a small stream flowing from the north which a beaver had dammed up, the pond formed would have been very similar in shape to the pond designed for Pinecote."[5] Old Strawberry Farm road ditches brought water from across the facility into this low area, which held water for part of the year. The Slough Exhibit, the connecting water body that would expand into the pond, was designed and placed to take advantage of the water flowing from these existing ditches. In order to make the pond seem larger than it would actually be, the designers crenulated the water edges into long fingers of water and land, and they also added islands. Blake wrote: "Islands are being used to increase the depth of views, and a shoreline is being made to gently flow past protruding clusters of pines and disappear behind them, to suggest a world of fantasy, magic, and curiosity. It is in the realm of the mind that the Piney Woods Lake will be created to appear larger in size than it actually is."[6]

The experience of seeing open water would be countered along the pond's length by being pulled into the "shaded mysteries of the swamp forest."[7] With further development of the lake's shape and configuration from Colin Franklin of Andropogon Associates, the proposed outline of the lake was mowed to study its shape and design.

Blake did not have a strong biological background, and he depended on those around him to explain what he saw. He envisioned the role of the ecological designer as that of a translator, and in 1984 he wrote, "It will be the role of the design to optimize the array of harmonious relationships needed to produce an experience of beauty, fostering a sense of place that satisfies the academic rigors of science while retaining the landscape character appropriate to its natural environments."[8] Andropogon staff recommended a ten-foot pond depth in order to extend the time before the pond would silt on its own. However, a soil coring revealed that six feet was the depth of the clay layer that would best support water.

Andropogon also developed the educational aspects of the pond, with ideas such as displaying aquatic plants that change in composition as the water depths increase. The Emergent Cove, a long bridge traversing open water, was designed to show a gradually increasing depth of water and its corresponding plant growth. This water edge provides visitors a walk through the six aquatic zones of a pond: swamp forest zone, shrub zone, emergent zone, floating-leaved plants zone, submerged plants zone, and the free-floating plants zone.

Another important aspect of the pond's configuration involved its construction. Typically, most ponds are small enough to be dug from along their edges with backhoes and equipment traversing the area, but the wet clay soils around this pond would exhibit the impacts of equipment for many years after construction. Arboretum designers wisely decided to dig the water body from inside the pond outline rather than outside, requiring them to accommodate the turning radius of dump trucks from the inside of the pond footprint. Blake was tasked with completing the final design and construction documents for the Aquatic Exhibit. The challenge in the design of the pond, as Blake would later note, would be to "mix all the ingredients in the correct proportions in order to dramatize the symbolic notion of water as a universal life-nurturing element appropriate to this time, place, and culture."[9] The pond was more than an aesthetic amenity; it exemplified life. This metaphor is represented in its surroundings: the reflections of trees, the colors of late afternoon, the mists of early morning, the scattering of raindrops, and as an aperture toward the heavens at night.

The surrounding trail, which would eventually be called the Pond Journey, was routed to take advantage of different existing features. Its conceptual narrative intended to tell the stories of the life cycles of a lake, how it ages, and how plants adapt to water, and to enable the visitor to experience the light and shade of aquatic edges. Andropogon suggested letting the pond water level fluctuate as seen in local water bodies, which would allow for new seed regeneration at its edges and prevent water stagnation. However, the arboretum managers would rarely lower the pond level due to the compromise in aesthetics. Mud banks do not create the majestic reflections that water can provide. Blake selected the locations of bridges and landings and their orientation to viewing corridors and community exhibits. A variety of decks and bridges would bring people across the water and islands to offer an assortment of wetland experiences.

Blake sought out the best minds available to help him resolve the pond design details. Landscape architect Hartley Fairchild had pond construction experience and offered his design and construction guidance. Robert Poore, a landscape architecture student at MSU, was also involved in the design discussions for Piney Woods Lake. He had just completed a wetlands course and was invited to make an ecological study of the lake for his final student project.[10] Poore had access to the construction drawings Andropogon had just completed. His work on detailed sections and plans for the aquatic plantings gave a visualization of how the newly constructed pond would be vegetated and its resulting plant succession. Poore gained much from the experience and incorporated his learning into designs for his own landscape architecture firm, Native Habitats. He remained a knowledgeable colleague of the Crosby Arboretum staff and Blake.

Meanwhile, the Master Plan for Pinecote was still being refined. The area that would become the Woodland Exhibit was last burned in 1982. Eight years later, when the arboretum opened full-time, these young woodlands were mostly large shrubby masses of holly and wax myrtle. Young pines, maples, and oaks were beginning to take root and form the future forest.

In 1990 Chris Wells and I worked with a contractor to mow tractorwide strips of the entire grid system at Pinecote. This caused the somewhat bizarre pattern of walking in straight lines through the emerging shrubs, and seeing a long axis cut through the brush. Wells and Blake wanted this done in order to be able to walk the grid lines of the entire arboretum east-west and north-south to note vegetation changes along the lines. Indicator plants, or plants found only in wetter or drier environments, were used to ascertain the area's soil moisture type. For example, the presence of gallberry holly (*Ilex glabra*) signified that the soil was slightly drier. Where a plant species denoted a transition, such as from wet to moist, a note along that line was made on the plan. Similar to interpolating soil types for soil maps, connections were made across the entire Interpretive Center. These plant-soil relationships guided the placement of plant communities at Pinecote. Blake noted this in his 1985 notebook: "The site and land are revealing the design."[11]

Before the pond was excavated and construction initiated, the shape of the pond was studied for about a year. This waiting period was another important design principle used at Crosby: do things softly and then learn from the experience. Blake called this studying the *nature* of nature, and used the analogy of how small incremental changes occur in cells before they are locked into a genetic code. Instead of building a permanent element without initial testing, it would be better to take time and make an interim impact, such as mowing an outline of a pond or putting in a temporary element, until its effects could be further studied and evaluated. Then adjustments to the final design can be made.

Ponds are not static environments; they change over time. The Piney Woods Lake exhibit was designed with the knowledge that it would silt-in through sedimentation processes and the decay of pond plants, advancing aquatic succession. It would take decades before the bottom of the pond would fill and ultimately become shallow. Trees would eventually colonize the edges and create a still, shaded swamp. Over time, even the water itself would disappear and the site drainage shift elsewhere, leaving behind only the remnants of cypress and gum trees. Chris Wells noted before the pond's construction, "The trick for the biologist will be to maintain the lake in a biologically sound manner; for the landscape architect, it will be to make an aesthetically pleasing display within the ecological constraints of the Piney Woods."[12]

Nearly thirty years after its construction, the Piney Woods Lake Exhibit is one of the most popular visitor exhibits at the Crosby Arboretum. Hardwood trees—gum, maple, and cypress—planted along its edges have now reached into the canopy of the older pines and are dispersing their own seeds and fruit. The pond's edges and bottom are filling with dense organic ooze as the siltation process is well under way. Numerous life forms have taken hold in the aquatic exhibits, none of which were added by people. Catfish, bass, and bluegill are readily seen, turtles occupy logs on sunny days, and numerous frog species fill the night air with their songs, blending with buzzing cicadas. The Piney Woods Lake Exhibit has provided new opportunities for life at the Crosby Arboretum and new ways for humans to interact with nature. And this is the brilliance of the arboretum's concept, as articulated by its planners and implemented by the arboretum board, and the essence of its significance: employ science to shape design and craft design to explain science.[13]

After completion of the pavilion and pond exhibits, the next task was to establish the main visitor entry. Andropogon conceptualized the design for a small parking facility and treated it as one of the exhibits from which visitors would encounter and learn. Public garden facilities typically have a large parking area easily accessible from a major road, and visitors immediately enter a center that acts as a controlled gateway to the outdoor exhibits. In this fashion, ticket sales and entry are streamlined and visitors can walk through a retail area upon exit. But Andropogon and Blake had a different idea. They knew that the exhibits at the Crosby Arboretum were subtle in nature. The nuances of the landscape change almost imperceptibly across much of the Piney

Woods landscape, except to the trained eye, and visitors hardly notice these delicate changes. So Blake decided to slow the visitor's pace. He reasoned that if people were traveling at interstate speeds to get to the arboretum, then slowing down to 35 miles per hour on a service road, and finally arriving at the parking area at 5 mph, that the brain would need time to adjust from these changing speeds to a walking pace. In one of the more contested design ideas for the arboretum, Blake placed the main parking area about 500 feet away from the visitor center and another 300 feet from the Pinecote Pavilion. This removed location enabled visitors to get a glimpse of the three major exhibit types along the way to the buildings—grassland, woodland, and wetland exhibits. In this way, even visitors coming just to attend a program in the center would be required to encounter the outdoor exhibits.

In the early days of the arboretum when the forest was just emerging, views from the parking area offered tantalizing glimpses of Pinecote Pavilion. These brief views were seen from various aspects along the Arrival and Pond Journeys, allowing the structure to serve as a visual reference point to the wayfarer. Jones would say of Pinecote Pavilion, "You catch glimpses, then it disappears, and then you catch glimpses again."[14] The idea of nature unfolding before the visitor was an important concept since the arboretum's early days. Board member Osmond Crosby made a visit to the International Garden Festival in Munich and discovered that the strongest exhibits had a similar sense of discovery.[15]

The visitors' parking area became the first designed exhibit located away from the Pavilion/Pond Journey nucleus, and it carried the same design motifs. Jones crafted the design of the large metal entrance gates to seamlessly match the colors and design of Pinecote Pavilion's metal fixtures. The brick walls are of the same color as the pavilion's floor, and the surrounding wooden fences repeat across the entire site, ensuring that design unity is maintained. The design of the Visitors Entrance Area was an important step in creating an integrated design and would set the tone for future endeavors.

THE MAJOR EXHIBITS OF PINECOTE

Design must serve as bridge between the perception of fact and emotive response.

—Edward L. Blake Jr., personal notebooks, 1986

As Pinecote's infrastructure was being refined in the arboretum's Master Plan, botanist Chris Wells continued to hone the plant community exhibit structure. To guide the plantings at the arboretum grounds, he devised descriptions for each of the plant community exhibits and compiled a list of plant species that occurred there or are typically found within that community. This list allowed arboretum managers opportunities to add interest and variety to the visitor's experience and became the guidelines for planting new species. The following is a description of the major Master Plan exhibits.

THE SAVANNA EXHIBIT

The decision to keep the eastern third of the facility at the main entrance in grassland presented visitors with a glimpse of the region's predominant historical landscape scene: the pine savanna. Since the 1940s, the entire arboretum property had been maintained as a pine plantation and regularly burned; thus the Savanna Exhibit was already in place. The linear nature of Pinecote's configuration offered a savanna view down the entire length of the arboretum, nearly half a mile. Historically, and

Early morning in the Savanna
Exhibit.

Photo by Ed Blake Jr., courtesy of Marilyn Blake

on larger natural area tracts, savannas offer long vistas in many directions. But for a
smaller site such as Pinecote, taking advantage of the arboretum's vertical axis was the
best opportunity for visitors to experience an extensive visual prospect.

Blake manipulated the edges of the Savanna Exhibit to be wide in portions (such as
at the Pitcher Plant Bog Exhibit) and narrow in others. This wavy form allowed visitors to experience the breadth of a grassland and have the feeling of being in a large
grassy sea. The narrow portions of the savanna, sometimes less than one hundred feet
wide, pinch in the open space and carve the Savanna Exhibit into a series of outdoor
rooms. This variety of spatial forms creates interest as one walks along the length of
the exhibit.

The arboretum's thirty-year management as a pine plantation allowed the savanna
grassland to heal from the rutted impacts of the Strawberry Farm days. Fire-adapted
herbaceous species typically found in savannas regained foothold, and though the site
was not high in species diversity, the exhibit area already somewhat resembled a typi-
cal pine savanna assemblage. Grasses, sedges, wildflowers, and sundews (*Drosera* spp.)

were in plentiful supply. Woody shrubs dominated the Savanna Exhibit when arboretum managers first began to work with it, and after intensive prescribed fire management had reduced the shrub dominance, the savanna featured more grasses and herbs once again. Fortunately, the site's historic fire management had suppressed invasive exotic woody species that otherwise would have presented more extensive challenges.

The use of prescribed fire to maintain exhibits was not common in the world of arboreta, except at facilities such as the University of Wisconsin Arboretum. Forestry managers use fire as a tool to enhance pine forest production, but such practices are rarely seen in botanic gardens. Leslie Sauer from Andropogon Associates wrote about Crosby's use of fire management: "Using innovative technologies such as prescribed burning, the Arboretum is pioneering the management of southeastern coastal plain landscapes in a gardenesque setting. This applied research as well as the growing collection of indigenous plants that is fully documented and monitored will be invaluable in the effort to restore local ecosystems and to develop a regionally appropriate landscape vocabulary."[1]

The Savanna Exhibit just after a prescribed burn.

Photo by Ed Blake Jr., courtesy of Marilyn Blake

In the early days, the arboretum utilized fire crews and equipment from the Crosby family's lumber operations. As a result, the fire management practices tended to mimic those used in local forestry applications. Burning typically would occur in the winter months when it was cooler for the workers and wind direction was steady. But south Mississippi land managers were well versed in the application of prescribed fire, and studies of its use in the landscape can be traced to the 1930s. Bill Platt, a fire ecologist at Louisiana State University, was knowledgeable in the historical fire records of the Deep South and was an early consultant to the Crosby Arboretum. Platt's studies showed that, historically, fires typically occurred in the summer months as opposed to winter prescribed burns. While it is not conclusive that growing-season fires (prescribed fire used during the warm growing months) are advantageous to pines, it is known that growing-season fires do provide benefit to some grasses and wildflowers.[2]

When Chris Wells conducted the first summer burn in the Savanna Exhibit, he noticed that something different happened: wiregrass (*Aristida* spp.) bloomed for the first time. This meant that savanna species responded to a variety of fire intensities and timings. This observation led to another important arboretum discovery: that the fire management of the Savanna Exhibit could be tailored to the needs of different species and colony locations.

The numerous pathways that cross the savanna landscape offer appealing views from particular vantage points. But the pathways also serve an important purpose as firebreaks, which are used to contain the edges of ground fires. These pathways are managed strips of ground from which fuel (brush and vegetation) has been removed. Many forestry operations will disk a line to expose bare earth to create a firebreak. When fire reaches the open ground, there is no fuel to burn and the fire stops. The gravel pathways of the arboretum double as firebreaks and were designed along the entire periphery of the Savanna Exhibit. The mosaic of grassland patches in the exhibit can be burned individually according to the needs of the species being managed within those patches. Following historic fire patterns in the southeastern United States, prescribed burning in Crosby's Savanna Exhibit typically occurs every three to five years. Visitors are allowed to watch the burn from a safe distance and trained volunteers often participate, allowing for enhanced public understanding and learning about the role of fire in the ecosystem.

The Pitcher Plant Bog Exhibit, located in the wettest portion of the savanna, is burned during the winter months. The winter burn is done more for aesthetic reasons than biological ones, since the new flowers and leaves of pitcher plants that emerge in the spring are most visually dramatic without the previous year's surrounding growth. This contextualizes how the Crosby Arboretum design and management combine scientific reality with aesthetic considerations. Plants respond to the management decisions made for their locations, and those choices may be based on either their scientific rationale or artistic merits.

Ideally, arboreta bridge environmental sciences with the arts; and they often exhibit management decisions somewhere between these two endeavors. Chris Wells once wrote that "this synthesis of art and science is ample demonstration of the need for order in our garden and a better understanding of Nature—both are truly taking place at The Crosby Arboretum."[3]

This blending also offers opportunity for a poetic interplay between a scientific description and artful expression. This is evident in the names that Blake gave on the Master Plan to different environmental zones of the savanna—the Clustered Pine Basin, Sphagnum Moss Flat, Pine Upland Flat, Slash Pine Lowland, Pine Woods Depression, Pineland Slope, Pitcher Plant Bog, and Longleaf Pine Dome.[4] These names were assigned by simply looking at that particular exhibit landscape and stating its predominant and most obvious feature. Art has played an important role at Pinecote, ranging from the permanent architectural features designed by Fay Jones to the temporary exhibitions of outdoor sculptures, glass art, and displays by craftsmen.

The area designated as the Longleaf Pine Rise Exhibit in the Master Plan already had a small cluster of longleaf pine trees in the early 1980s. The few existing trees, however, only minimally conveyed the dramatic majesty these forests can evoke. To increase the exhibit's sensory potential, dozens of longleaf pine saplings were planted to create a strong repetition of pine trunks. This repeated linear effect of blackened pine trunks created a lilting rhythm for the viewer and clarified the area as a distinct and different place. Also, new species were planted in its wildflower understory to improve the density and visibility of showier herbaceous species, including pine lily (*Lilium catesbaei*), sunflowers (*Helianthus* spp.), and meadow beauty (*Rhexia* spp.). The Longleaf Pine Rise Exhibit at Pinecote could never rival the sheer size and scope of

Young longleaf pines shimmer in the autumn landscape, 2006.

Photo by Ed Blake Jr., courtesy of Marilyn Blake

the older longleaf pine forest at Talowah, located about forty miles north of the arboretum. But it can provide a small glimpse of how that forest feels. Arboretum planners knew that helping visitors become more knowledgeable and interested is the first step in long-term environmental conservation.

A fine example of enhancing the site's visual appeal can be seen in the Pitcher Plant Bog Exhibit, located in the extreme southern portion of the Savanna Exhibit. There were few pitcher plants growing there in the early days of the arboretum, and an area just across the road featured several acres of pitcher plants densely packed together—an incredible visual display. The absence of pitcher plants at the arboretum may have been due to its previous farming use, which would have destroyed the original colonies. Thousands of acres of these specialized wetlands along the Gulf Coast were decimated through the cessation of prescribed burning, the implementation of drainage ditches, overgrazing, or insensitive development. Luckily, bogs can be readily restored by removing the encroaching woodland and returning the much-needed fire. Reinstating prescribed burning at Pinecote and transplanting rescued species into the bogs has produced successful results.

Beginning in the late 1980s, numerous bog rescues were conducted at local areas undergoing development. With permission from landowners, hundreds of shovel-sized scoops of bog plants were dug and transplanted into the Savanna Exhibit. One advantage of this method is that in addition to the pitcher plant rhizomes, many associated plant species were also transplanted. There is a danger, however, of bringing in unwanted, non-native species together with desired native plants. In one growing season, native plants such as grass pink orchids (*Calopogon tuberosus*) and meadow beauties (*Rhexia*) joined the pitcher plants and other carnivorous species in a stunning visual display that is now one of the arboretum's most popular exhibits. This colorful feature will only continue to expand through additional plantings in time. Children are fascinated by carnivorous plants, and adults marvel at their beauty.

The Pitcher Plant Bog Exhibit was largely inspired by the Hillside Bog natural area. At Hillside, there is a transition in landscape types from an upland longleaf pine area, to a pitcher plant bog, down to a low sweetbay–swamp tupelo–swampbay woodland. Pinecote was designed with an existing upland longleaf pine rise transitioning to the Pitcher Plant Bog Exhibit, then down to a wet woodland along the Piney Woods Lake. A planting of black titi (*Cliftonia monophylla*) was placed near the lake's edge to reflect the exact same community as at Hillside Bog.

In the 1990s the author designed and built, along with Crosby staff and volunteers, a 400-foot wooden walkway that traverses the bog and lightly sits upon the wetland soils. A local timber company donated the wood for the walkway, which gives visitors the opportunity to examine the bog from within the exhibit. There is a 20-foot-wide square "research plot" on the walkway's surface, enabling visitors to examine the minute plants below. The Pitcher Plant Bog Exhibit demonstrates that an educational, functioning, and appealing display can facilitate new understandings of the ecology of a particular plant community. While Crosby's pitcher plant exhibit does not rival the breadth of the twenty acres of densely packed pitcher plants at Hillside Bog, it does allow visitors to experience a concentrated version of a bog ecosystem.

THE WOODLAND EXHIBITS

Existing moisture conditions throughout the site determined the types of Pinecote's Woodland Exhibits. Dry rises not maintained by fire were identified as suitable for the Beech-Magnolia Exhibit, and would be planted with American beech (*Fagus grandifolia*), southern magnolia, and live oak (*Quercus virginiana*). The majority of Pinecote's soil types are moist and were deemed suitable for the Transitional Hardwoods Exhibit. This forest type will support a deciduous forest of red oaks (*Quercus falcata*), white oaks (*Quercus alba*), and red maples (*Acer rubrum* var. *drummondii*). The wettest woodlands were slated to become the Sweetbay–Swamp Tupelo–Swampbay Exhibit. These are common local wetland communities composed of sweetbay magnolia, tupelo gum (*Nyssa sylvatica* var. *biflora*), and swampbay trees (*Persea palustris*). Approximately 150 plant species native to the Pearl River Drainage Basin are suitable for display and planting at Pinecote. The numbers and types of species vary according to each exhibit's specific designation.

Two-thirds of Pinecote's acreage is now covered by woodlands that were established in 1982, the date of the last comprehensive site burn. The process to establish the forest exhibit was simple: managers stopped burning and disturbing the landscape, and within a few years, woody plants dominated the once-grassy plain. The Woodland Exhibits area was primarily a shrub and young tree thicket when the site opened full-time to the public in 1990. The first shrub and tree species that appeared under the pine overstory were sun-loving plants that had been suppressed for years under the frequent burning regime—wax myrtles (*Morella cerifera*), hollies (*Ilex* spp.), red maples, sweetbay magnolias, pines, and many other plants native to the pine flatwoods.

These trees and shrubs formed a massive thicket across the Woodland Exhibits when the arboretum first opened, and personnel were challenged to explain the value of this tangled shrub mass to increasing audiences. However, the trees grew quickly and the Woodland Exhibits area began to resemble a young forest by the end of the 1990s, mostly due to abundant rainfall and the mild Gulf Coast climate. In twenty years, the sun-loving wax myrtles and hollies began to die out from the increasing shade provided by the faster-growing trees, and the forest understory began to open.

Andropogon Associates maintained in 1988 that "Pinecote is not the place where scientists observe but do not interfere. This stance is appropriate only for the natural areas, and not for a place where the public is invited to enjoy the outdoor exhibits."[5] Pruning, or plant shaping techniques, would be an important part of the management at Pinecote. A visiting Chinese garden scholar, Dr. C. Z. Tang, first shaped the plants along Pinecote's pathways. During his short stay in 1987, Dr. Tang utilized his expert skills in bonsai along the newly constructed Pond Journey. Some of the plants that he selected to manipulate served as focal points, while others acted as mass-forming elements. Because of the fast growth of the plants, many of his pruning efforts were obscured within a season. It would take a long-term pruning effort to maintain this management method. But it did show to the public, perhaps for the first time in an arboretum setting, that a successional landscape can be viewed as "ornamental" on its own terms.

Over the years, the Crosby staff and I have spent many hours shaping the pathway edges in a similar fashion, with pruners and a pole saw. I have learned how to see strong, inherent forms that exist within the plants, mostly by utilizing the principles I learned in art classes. To see clearly the vertical expressiveness of a pine thicket, I removed the angled stems of wax myrtle or the greenbriar vines (*Smilax* sp.) that covered them. To expose the starburst stems of a wax myrtle thicket, I simply removed the pines. Repetition of form is a design element that is readily achieved in the pine flatwood.

Other woody plant species had other inherent configurations: blueberry stems arched gracefully into semi-circular patterns, titi stems snaked sinuously with orange peeling bark, and black gums with horizontal limbs cantilevered across the pathways. Sometimes pruning was most effective to expose some unseen feature of a plant, such as the horizontal banding of black cherry bark or the bright green moss accumulating at the base of a pine tree, or to showcase a short-lived colony of mushrooms. Pruning in this fashion is similar to building a theater set that allows the players of nature to dance across its stage. At other times, it seems best to leave a sprawling greenbriar vine to envelop its neighboring shrubs, inciting awe and respect for this thorny, entangled mass that provides a sumptuous display of midsummer fruit. This deliberate exposure of the richness of form, color, texture, pattern, line, color, contrast, and harmony takes advantage of what is already present in the landscape—at no cost. It is simply a matter of revealing the inner form, *judiciously pruning when necessary.*

Such landscape editing was particularly effective along the Pond Journey. In the southeastern United States, natural wetlands typically have few evergreen trees and instead have a deciduous fringe. This was very noticeable along the edge of the pond, where the fast-growing slash and loblolly pines resembled green rockets shooting through the emerging shrubs. By simply removing these errant pines, the pond took on a whole new character, color, and feeling, resembling wetlands more commonly found in the region.

Another important aspect of pruning was to control how light fell within the exhibits. Exhibit areas that were thicker and darker due to a dense understory were opened in select places to allow light to penetrate as a focal point. Andropogon's Carol Franklin recalled in 2011 that she observed from Russel Wright's garden how "to create these special places that are spotlighted as if a stage set."[6] All of us who have worked at the arboretum have learned how landscape editing can manipulate the design elements of place.

In addition to allowing woodland succession to occur onsite, designers intended that the arboretum be planted. Franklin spelled this out in 1988 in a reminder letter to the arboretum: "because Pinecote is the first introduction of the visitor to the beauty of the landscapes of the region it is desirable to widen the vocabulary beyond plant communities certain to be found on the site, to include those plant communities that might only rarely be found in similar conditions. Stretching the potential plant communities slightly beyond strict scientific accuracy allows Pinecote to exhibit more diversity, without distorting the qualities of the site."[7]

The question of plant provenance (place of origin) became part of a considerable debate for the arboretum board. Purists wanted to feature only the plant species that were already present onsite, while others pondered introducing species from farther up the Pearl River Drainage Basin. Tom Dodd III, a respected native plant nurseryman from Semmes, Alabama, was involved in these early plant discussions. He recommended that the arboretum utilize native plant species that were propagated from local sources and to add them according to the specifics of the place they were planted. Dodd recalled recently that he advocated for site managers to remain open and flexible, adding that "a lot of these plants haven't read the book."[8]

Some of the first planting efforts at Pinecote, after the Pond Journey construction was completed in 1986, were conducted by using a species list developed for each of the exhibits. In theory, these plants would be suitable for planting in habitats with specific soil moisture and soil types. In practice, many species adapted quite well into the young emerging woodland, but as Dodd had wisely observed, a few sensitive species would not.

Some tree types such as dogwood (*Cornus florida*) and silverbell (*Halesia diptera*) did not survive more than a few years when planted in the Beech-Magnolia Exhibit at Pinecote. The effort, based on the idea that the slightly elevated topographic rises would support the drier species, did not take into account the existing soil texture. The fine silty-clay soil at Pinecote with its high water table stays wetter for a longer period than the sandy-loamy upland soils where dogwoods grow. Plus, dogwood and silverbell are not as tolerant and hardy as some other native plants. Species that did not perform well at Pinecote's exhibits were dropped from the plant lists, evincing another important principle used to manage the exhibits: if it is appropriate to the plant community and it survives, it belongs; if it dies, it doesn't. Plant species that were more tolerant of Pinecote's soil and moisture type were planted much more frequently. Southern magnolia, baldcypress (*Taxodium distichum*), and spruce pine (*Pinus glabra*) were found to adapt to a wide range of conditions at Pinecote.

Arboretum staff planted canopy tree species in each exhibit type in order to shape the composition of Pinecote's forest and to allow visitors to more easily see the differences between habitat types. Live oaks were planted into slight rises as nearby forests demonstrate, and cypress trees were installed thickly at the swampy pond edges. Repeated plantings of similar tree types were commonly used when installing plants in the exhibits. In the Cypress Cove Exhibit, there were a few existing pond cypress trees (*Taxodium ascendens*) growing along the edge of an old road ditch. The decision was made to install several dozen pond and baldcypress trees to emphasize the experience and heighten the drama of walking through the edge of a cypress swamp. These cypress trees, now mature, drop their seeds to the soil below, and a new generation of trees has since sprouted. Throughout, birds, mammals, wind, water, and people now carry the fruit from these planted trees to new places, both on the arboretum property and to the community outside its borders.

While Pinecote's planting palette and locations were defined by the botanists, it took an artist's eye to articulate the aesthetics of where they should occur along the pathways. Franklin described this blending of art and science as a suggestion for planting: "At the edge of the pond, understory trees such as *Halesia,* lean out over the water in a red maple/ash lowland forest to form a flowering edge, in early spring, and in the gaps in the dark cypress swamps, sedges and delicate orchids colonize the stumps of old fallen trees."[9] As the woody plants grew in the emerging woodland, board members grew concerned about the decreasing numbers of flowers along Pinecote's pathways. Few wildflowers bloomed in the shade provided by the emerging shrubs and trees in the Woodland Exhibits. The ground layer of ferns, shade-tolerant wildflowers, and ground vines was not yet planted. Over time, however, colonies of these shade plants were added to become established into masses. The board was reminded by Andropogon that this new form of arboretum could not just make colorful pathway additions, but instead,

> for art to reflect accurately the latest, best, scientific information, it requires scientific information that is translated or translatable into PATTERN. Most modern ecologists are into population dynamics, however, species numbers and lists although extremely useful for other reasons, do not lead to inspired ecological design. Despite the fact that the concept of "plant community" is a more arbitrary and elusive description we feel it can be translated into a more compelling visual image.[10]

After the new exhibits shifted from savanna to woodland, the animal species present on the site changed as well. Fish and amphibians readily colonized the newly constructed water bodies, likely by wading birds such as herons and egrets that carry fish and frog eggs on their long legs. These were soon followed by aquatic mammals and birds migrating in, such as river otters, beavers, and ducks. Grassland animals including Henslow sparrows, bluebirds, bobwhite quail, and terrestrial snakes maintained a foothold in the savanna, even with reduced grassland acreage. The woodlands added more animal diversity, and evidence of deer, bobcat, coyote, and red fox became increasingly apparent. As the emerging oaks matured on the site and began to produce acorns, a primary wildlife food, squirrels and other woodland species soon became established. An increased diversity of habitat resulted in a rich assemblage of wildlife species. Many Crosby Arboretum visitors have an interest in observing wildlife, and the addition of more animal evidence to the exhibits enhanced programs and visitation.

The arboretum's budget did not allow for extensive plant purchases, yet many thousands of saplings were added to the exhibits. Honor and memorial tree donations supported the purchase of larger plant installations, and free seedlings acquired from state conservation organizations added new species to the property. Plant rescues were conducted in area bogs and woodlands threatened with development. All species types added to the arboretum's exhibits, together with dates and locations, were documented in the arboretum's permanent accession records.

The mission statement of any facility guides its major efforts and management actions. As the Crosby Arboretum is dedicated to preserving and displaying the native plants and their communities of the Pearl River Drainage Basin, all of its education programs, exhibits, and management activities would strive to support that goal. However, this is often easier said than done. Exotic invasive plants run rampant through the south Mississippi landscape. Chinese privet (*Ligustrum sinense*), Japanese honeysuckle (*Lonicera japonica*), and Chinese tallow trees (*Sapium sebiferum*) are just a few of the dozens of exotic species that have escaped across Mississippi's lands. Some, such as privet, were introduced as garden plants and rapidly spread from bird dispersal of their seeds. Others, such as cogon grass (*Imperata cylindrica*), were accidentally introduced and their seed distributed by wind. Because of the aggressive nature of these species and favorable growing conditions in the southern landscape, invasive plants have spread far and wide. Exotic species have few natural controls such as diseases, viruses, or predators in the ecosystem. As a result, these aggressive plants can outcompete native plants for space, nutrients, water, and light. Unfortunately, even with federally funded exotic invasive management programs by the U.S. Fish and Wildlife Service and other agencies, these plants perpetuate in the landscape.

A native plant arboretum is akin to an ark floating in a changing world. It contains a high level of native biodiversity but is continually influenced by its surroundings. Birds, wind, flooding, and a variety of animals can carry the seeds of plants for many miles. If left unmonitored or unchecked, species can spread fast, especially in a small garden of sixty-four acres. It takes diligent efforts to combat invasive plants, and this is especially critical at a native plant facility. The presence of exotic species in a center that teaches about native plants can create confusion in the visiting public. The configuration of Pinecote, with its long borders, narrow interior, and highly disturbed edges, is disposed to continual exotic plant invasion, and requires constant vigilance to monitor for new outbreaks.

Years ago, I determined that an integrated pest-management strategy was the most sustainable solution to manage the needs of the arboretum. While insecticides, fungicides, fertilizers, and other horticulture quick-fixes have their place with proper usage in gardens, they were not used at Pinecote for the thousands of new plantings and their subsequent care. Irrigation systems were not implemented in the landscape exhibits, and newly installed plants, at most, received a full bucket of pond water and a silent wish for good luck. The native species planted in the exhibits during the winter months (recommended as the best time to plant in the area) did quite well without supplemental care, except in times of extreme drought.

An underlying principle of the arboretum's management strategy was to find out how nature solved problems and then adopt that method. Once, several dozen large river birch trees that had just been planted along the pond's edge developed a severe aphid problem on the new leaves. The majority of leaves turned sickly, and the trees' survival was threatened. Realizing that predators were missing from the equation, I purchased ladybugs from a mail-order source to eat the aphids. In short order the ladybugs solved the problem, and in subsequent years when the aphids once again appeared to consume the new growth, the now-established ladybugs kept them under control. Utilizing such systems-based approaches was more effective at Crosby than quick fixes and enabled us to practice what we preach about natural sustainability, to demonstrate to our visitors the efficacy of such approaches, and also to save on maintenance budgets.

The Crosby Arboretum does not feature horticultural specimens as do many botanic gardens; instead, it focuses on developing healthy and viable ecosystems. Ecosystem approaches to management employ a system of checks and balances, of predator and prey, as the above ladybug/aphids interaction represents. This organic approach at a public garden facility provides the added benefit of a learning occasion for the visiting public. Creating teaching opportunities and displaying management approaches for maintaining healthy and resilient landscapes are the most valuable services of any public educational facility.

The arboretum's Woodland Exhibits will mature in places and continue to change and shift through time. As the hardwood understory transitions to be the overstory, the forest will change to a deeply shaded environment, and new shade garden design opportunities will arise. Storms and hurricanes will occasionally open the canopy in some places to the sun, pines will once again colonize, and new successional exhibits will again be born.

AQUATIC EXHIBITS

Prior to the arboretum's development, agricultural ditches and bogs were the only existing wetlands at Pinecote. With the addition of the Piney Woods Lake and other aquatic exhibits at the site's center, water has become a prominent feature at Pinecote. This is highly appropriate as the property's primary drainage corridor already occurred at this central zone.

Nearly ten percent of Pinecote's land was proposed to become wetland exhibits in the arboretum's Master Plan. These exhibits included the Piney Woods Lake, Gum Pond, Wetland Edge, Slough, Savanna Inlet, and Cypress Ditch. The Piney Woods Lake (also called the Beaver Pond) was the first of the aquatic exhibits to be constructed and is the largest, extending nearly two acres in size. This broad wetland will maintain its youthful character for some time due to its large size and plentiful sunlight. As the surrounding trees mature, the edges of the pond will resemble a shaded swamp, and only the middle of the pond will receive a narrow ribbon of light. Decaying leaves and vegetation will settle into the pond and eventually provide the substrate for wetland trees to establish, and the sunny pond will transition, one day, into a shady cypress-gum swamp.

The Slough Exhibit

The Slough Exhibit was constructed in 1985 at the same time as the Piney Woods Lake. Sloughs are narrow, small water channels similar to bayous or small rivers, and the Slough Exhibit is often stagnant and flows very slowly. The Slough Exhibit was constructed to collect water from the ditches that drain the north end of the site to feed the water into Piney Woods Lake. The Slough also leads visitors from the entry toward Pinecote Pavilion and the Piney Woods Lake.

Cypress trees planted in the early 1990s now blend into the surrounding wetland forest, 2006.

Photo by Ed Blake Jr., courtesy of Marilyn Blake

The Cypress Ditch Exhibit, a remnant agricultural element from the Strawberry Farm, is located south of the Piney Woods Lake and serves as the overflow from the pond. As the majority of Pinecote's drainage flows to this southern end, the agricultural ditch has historically been a wetland drainage channel and already had a presence of older sweetbay magnolia and cypress trees. Other than the development of pathways and viewing stations, there were no modifications to this existing wetland environment.

The Gum Pond Exhibit

Gum ponds, found in the Gulf Coastal Plain, are shallow-water forested wetlands with one distinguishing characteristic: they are predominantly populated by black gum trees (*Nyssa sylvatica* var. *biflora*). Neither always wet nor dry, gum ponds occupy a place between extremes. They usually dry in the summer from heat and evaporation but become flooded in the winter. In the coldest season, they are a strange and wonderful wetland filled with silver-barked gum trees rising from dark organic waters.

Gum swamp forests are rare in Mississippi owing to extensive draining for agricultural purposes and from impacts of road construction projects. They are listed as a threatened wetland by the Mississippi Department of Wildlife, Fisheries & Parks. Twenty-six rare species of wildlife utilize gum pond habitats, such as frogs and amphibians—including one of the most endangered amphibians in North America, the Mississippi gopher frog. Very few Mississippi gopher frog populations are left in the state, and they use gum ponds as their primary breeding pools.[11]

Anchoring the northern end of the arboretum site, the Gum Pond Exhibit collects and stores water from the upper end of Pinecote. The exhibit was originally conceived as a one-acre pond encircled by wetland trees. Similar to Piney Woods Lake, the proposed site was already a wet area, and fortunately, it already had a number of black gum trees.

The Gum Pond Exhibit and the connecting Forested Stream Channel Exhibit were the last large-scale excavation projects designated on Pinecote's Master Plan. In spring 2010, I taught a graduate course dedicated to resolving the design and construction of the Gum Pond Exhibit. Grants were available for wetland habitat construction through the federal Five-Star Restoration Program, and the Crosby Arboretum Foundation submitted a proposal to fund the construction of the pond. The grant for construction of the Gum Pond Exhibit was awarded later that year, and we then began an intensive study to resolve the exhibit design details.

The graduate class researched wetland ecology and visited several natural gum ponds in south Mississippi. Students measured water depths, documented the wetland configurations, noted the plant community types and species, and sketched and photographed the landscape. These observations were summarized and used to reevaluate the Gum Pond Exhibit plan. The background studies resulted in some notable design changes to the gum pond as originally laid out in the arboretum's Master Plan, including reducing the overall size and depth of the excavation. Many of these changes were made to accommodate wildlife uses of the pond and to more clearly interpret ideas to the general public. The overall concept driving the design of the Gum Pond Exhibit was to create "a small jewel in the forest."

The Gum Pond Exhibit six months after construction, 2011.

Photo by author

The Gum Pond Exhibit was conceived as the antithesis of the Piney Woods Lake Exhibit. While the Piney Woods Lake was large, open, and had deep water, the Gum Pond would be small, forested, and shallow. The lake remains permanently flooded because it has a supplemental water feed, but the gum pond would be ephemeral and continually change in water depth. Following a student design charrette, I condensed the students' exhibit ideas into a final Gum Pond Exhibit Master Plan in the summer of 2010.

Tragically, Ed Blake was diagnosed with cancer at this time and was unable to participate in the design resolution because of his medical treatments. However, he was able to review the final plans and visit the exhibit site with the project contractor. Ed would not survive to see the completed pond. Even though he beat cancer, he passed away that summer from a massive heart attack. The excavation for the Gum Pond Exhibit was completed two months later and expertly executed by local construction contractor Daniel Broome. Garrett Newton, a landscape architecture student at Louisiana State University, interned for a semester at Crosby Arboretum and assisted in the development of the exhibit. True to the arboretum's incremental process, the architectural and pathway elements for the exhibit area were completed much later, allowing ample time for reflection and adjustment. Dr. Timothy Schauwecker, associate professor in the landscape architecture department at MSU, conducted vegetation studies of the exhibit. Schauwecker recorded the vegetation that emerged from the newly constructed edges of the pond and charted its progress.

While the site's abundant black gum understory already surrounded this new water body, arboretum staff continued to strengthen its vision as a gum pond. Within the first two years of the pond's creation, hundreds of young black gum trees were densely planted along and in the pond's edges. As these trees mature, they will help to convey the character of this wetland type even more, and their dense branches will create a sparkling silvery edge to this striking wetland.

The Forested Stream Exhibit

Small forested streams are common wetland features in the Piney Woods landscape. As these narrow bodies collect water and distribute it to larger creeks and streams, they play an important role in the health of local watersheds. Some of the associated features along small forested streams are equally important, such as the lowland depressions that occur adjacent to these creeks. One such Coastal Plain wetland, the small-stream swamp forest, is considered endangered in Mississippi due to historic widespread declines and losses caused by fragmentation.[12] Habitat fragmentation occurs when another land use such as a road or a development interrupts or reduces the original size. Two rare amphibian species are indigenous to the small-stream swamp forest: the one-toed amphiuma (*Amphiuma pholeter*) and the river frog (*Rana heckscheri*). Both are considered critically imperiled and at risk of extinction.

The Forested Stream Exhibit hydrologically connects the Gum Pond Exhibit to the existing Slough and Piney Woods Lake. It incorporates the agricultural ditches of the old Strawberry Farm and changes them into an exhibit that reflects the small streams of the area. This exhibit becomes the central water spine of Pinecote. As with the gum pond design, Pinecote's Master Plan outlined the general concept for the exhibit, but the redesign took into account new data and updated site information.

The design of the Forested Stream Exhibit and its accompanying 4.1 acres of land was, like that of the gum pond, explored initially as a graduate-school class project. The class examined small forested streams in south Mississippi and researched their ecology. Several associates from Jones and Jones, a noted ecological landscape architecture firm from Seattle, visited with the class in Mississippi and conducted a charrette for the exhibit's design. Taking the class's design ideas for the wetland exhibit, I spent the next summer realigning and laying the stream channel according to the specifics of the site. The design incorporates a broad and flowing feeling as the water exits from the Gum Pond Exhibit and transitions to a tight and twisting channel farther down. The stream channel path snakes sinuously around the trunks of large trees and reflects the streamside vegetation. Unique regional forested bottomland types such as the white cedar swamp will be planted and interpreted. The white cedar swamp is a shallow wetland rarely found in Mississippi and dominated by Atlantic white cedar (*Chamaecyparis thyoides*). This white cedar exhibit will be abstracted in form and planted in the area. Incorporating these unique wetland communities offers an opportunity to educate the visiting public on landscapes that are special to their region. A Five-Star restoration grant was awarded for the construction of the exhibit, and it was built in 2012.

BIOLOGICAL FILTER SYSTEM

The Crosby Arboretum Interpretive Center is located just outside of Picayune's city limits, a cause for some dismay during its early development as there were no city water or sewer connections available for use on the property. A deep-water well (over 1,000 feet) was dug to an artesian source that would supply ample water. The artesian well is sulfurous in odor and taste but is otherwise good drinking water. Yet with lack of a city sewer system, the problem remained of how to handle restroom needs.

Fortunately, the arboretum site is located near the National Aeronautics and Space Administration's (NASA) John C. Stennis Space Center, which was built in the 1960s.

Forested Stream Exhibit, four
months after construction,
2013.

Constructed to test new rocket engines, this facility had numerous engineers and scientists on staff. Among them was Dr. B. C. Wolverton, an engineer who developed and tested ecological life-support systems. NASA was interested in learning how the absorptive qualities of plants and root microbes could help minimize toxic chemicals in living areas for long-term space habitation. Dr. Wolverton assessed air quality within an early constructed "biohome," a sealed living structure made with the same synthetic materials as found on space flights.[13] Volunteer subjects lived in the biohome environment for brief periods, and the addition of interior plants was found to reduce airborne pollutants. The subjects' wastes were also collected and recycled through the biohome's wastewater treatment facility, and were then used for plant fertilizer.

When the Crosby Arboretum opened full-time in 1990, installing a septic field was impossible due to the wetland nature of the soils. Dr. Wolverton agreed to consult on the technical aspects of the design of a vegetated rock filter that would process and clean the restroom waste. A vegetated rock filter is a subsurface flow system that uses the root microbes of plants to break down organic nutrients. After I began my tenure at Crosby Arboretum, this became one of my first design projects, and I resolved the construction plans and details.

The long gravel treatment trench for the blackwater stream that flowed from the septic tank was designed in a curving fashion to fit into surrounding exhibits. A distinct challenge was to find the types of plants that would grow in such a gravel trench. Native plants added to the filter trench would have to be adapted to extreme wet conditions in winter and very dry conditions in summer. The answer for the planting came from studying the gravel beds along a local creek. We identified native rushes and grasses that thrived in either flood or drought conditions, and we selected and planted these species in the vegetated filter. In the context of the Piney Woods Lake Exhibit, the filter system area became an open grassy wetland that abutted the forest edge. Water quality tests conducted after installation of the vegetated filter system showed it to functionally clean the organic stream from the water. Vegetated rock filter systems require maintenance to prevent woody shrubs and trees from establishing within the filter, and avoiding excessive siltation is also important.

The development of the Crosby biological filter system is a prime example of successfully applying Andropogon's suggestion to consider a broad array of options and take time in problem solving. Testing potential solutions and applying the information gained is an adaptive management process that is often used in conservation or the management of natural areas. Lance Gunderson, a professor of environmental studies at Emory University, observed in 1999 that adaptive management "acknowledges that managed resources will always change as a result of human intervention, that surprises are inevitable, and that new uncertainties will emerge. Active learning is the way in which the uncertainty is winnowed."[14]

7

AN ARBORETUM GROWS

The most critical and difficult task of the programs at the Crosby
Arboretum will be to complement the living landscape of the exhibits at the
Strawberry Farm site and the natural areas.

—Andropogon Associates, "Outline for Developing the First-Year
Program of the Crosby Arboretum," 1983

The Crosby Arboretum began a few public education programs while the young site was being developed in the mid-1980s. The facility offered limited tours for local groups, but as Blake wrote in his notebook from 1985, "As a child grows up, it acquires a huge amount of information before putting it to use. Is the Arboretum a similar analogy?"[1] Blake proposed to spend this time studying how people used the site and in documenting its resources, rather than investing much time in its early program development.

Learning from Nature children's program.

Photo courtesy of Crosby Arboretum

The arboretum's first public education efforts focused on the region's rich cultural heritage. Communication Arts, the Crosby Arboretum's graphic design firm, had established the arboretum's identity early by developing its logo and quarterly newsletter formats. The firm was also com-

99

missioned to develop the arboretum's first poster exhibit, "Man and the Land," which traced the history of the arboretum's lands and portrayed the region's historical context. The "Man and the Land" exhibit displayed human dependence on and sustenance from the Piney Woods ecosystem.

Discussions about programming continued with Andropogon Associates, and in 1986 Leslie Sauer suggested the educational focus—to learn from and center on the land. Blake wrote in 1986 that the Piney Woods was the unsung hero of American culture and that the arboretum's efforts should celebrate its importance. The area's emphasis on forestry, agriculture, mineral extraction, and urbanization creates a strong relationship of people to the land, and conversely, shows how the land adapts and changes in response to human activities. Blake and other early planners determined that programs would concentrate on "what living in this area is all about, and how to train people to become land managers."[2] The Piney Woods focus provided a familiar topic to a local audience and would promote a greater understanding of place. Offering environmental education tailored to the public's immediate surroundings encourages greater appreciation for their environmental context.

The arboretum opened full-time in 1990 with an ambitious program schedule. Because of the local and regional nature of the arboretum, programs and events were specific to place. Local artists displayed their work or performed dance, speakers discussed pertinent environmental issues, and staff taught the public about the arboretum's displays and its green technologies—all under the sheltering roof of Pinecote Pavilion. One home-grown program is Strawberries and Cream, held annually during the strawberry season in March. Begun in 1986 as a way to honor Pinecote's agricultural history, the event draws hundreds of visitors who come to eat strawberries and cream and enjoy an afternoon of entertainment. Other annual events that celebrate the local cultural and natural heritage include the Piney Woods Heritage Festival, native plant sales, Forge Day (which includes demonstrations of traditional metal-smithing techniques), Wildlife Day, nature camps, entomology festivals, classes that offer approaches to stewardship, natural landscapes and native plant tours, and many other environmental education events. Patricia Drackett, director of the Crosby Arboretum, noted that "while many persons who visit the Crosby Arboretum are aware of our history and mission, we also constantly seek innovative ways for attracting first-time visitors to experience the site. Our programs and events offer the public a diversity of educational activities that explore nature and provide opportunities to learn about native plants and their use in the home landscape."[3]

The educational program meeting in 1986 with Andropogon Associates also brought a revisioning and sharpening of the Crosby Arboretum's mission statement. It now read that the arboretum would be concerned with "the preservation and display of plants and their communities [native] to the Pearl River Drainage Basin."[4] The inclusion of the term *communities* would distinguish the arboretum's efforts from those of other conservation organizations that concentrated efforts on the preservation of individual species.

In the early 1990s, Crosby Arboretum offices were located in three different cities to accommodate individual staff needs. An effort was made by Anne Bradburn, then the Crosby Foundation president, to gather all of the employees together on the arboretum site. This resulted in a series of "temporary" (manufactured) buildings that provided staff offices, a gift shop, and a small educational program space. Crosby's first employee, Chris Wells, left in 1993 to work at the National Wetland Center in Lafayette, Louisiana.

The Crosby Arboretum also saw development in the area of plant propagation with the addition of a greenhouse. The arboretum was becoming increasingly reliant on income generated from programs and plant sales. In an effort to save on plant-purchase costs for the exhibits and for retail sales, a greenhouse facility donated by an arboretum member was constructed in the Restoration Center (support) area. The arboretum hired a full-time horticulturist to begin propagation efforts through a local grant. With the addition of the greenhouse, the Restoration Center began to grow as a public education area as well as a service and storage zone. In subsequent years, a children's garden was constructed in the same area, followed by a 4-H garden and a butterfly garden. These gardens allow opportunities for teaching the next generation of gardeners.

Blake left the Crosby Arboretum in 1994 and taught for a year as a visiting lecturer at the Harvard Graduate School of Design. With his wife Marilyn as partner, he then started his own landscape architecture firm in Hattiesburg and called it the Landscape Studio. His years spent at Pinecote and the lessons gained became the basis for his new projects in the state and elsewhere. Blake would create many award-winning landscapes and train a new generation of young landscape architects through his studio. Until his death in 2010, Blake remained an integral contributor and valued consultant to the Crosby Arboretum Foundation board.

After Blake's departure, a series of pivotal events unfolded at the arboretum. A new director, Larry Pardue, brought his experience of fundraising from other southeastern botanic garden institutions. Pardue would focus his efforts on increasing membership and programming and on income generation during his short tenure. He surmised that if the arboretum was going to continue as a private, nonprofit entity, it would have to substantially expand its ticket receipts and income. Realizing that the current acreage and Master Plan constraints limited potential fundraising avenues and exhibits, he pursued the acquisition of an additional forty acres adjacent to the Interpretive Center. With this added land, Pardue could develop ideas outside of the Master Plan yet not impact the original design. As the Crosby board completed the land purchase, a new organizational arrangement was in the works.

THE CROSBY ARBORETUM, MISSISSIPPI STATE UNIVERSITY EXTENSION

By the mid-1990s, it was apparent to the board of directors that fundraising was not in place to continue as a private foundation. The Crosby Arboretum did not have a permanent endowment and would have to find another way to sustain itself. After discussions with several universities and careful consideration of its options, the Crosby Arboretum Foundation merged with the state entity that had provided its major guidance all along, MSU. Fortuitously, MSU was in the midst of a capital campaign, and Crosby Arboretum was offered as a gift to the state by the Crosby board. The Crosby Arboretum board negotiated the merger in June 1997.[5]

MSU's presence across the state falls into five administrative regions, and the arboretum would be administered directly by the Coastal Research and Extension Cen-

Dr. Donald Zacharias (*left*), fifteenth president of MSU, and Doug Wilds (*right*), president of the Crosby Arboretum board of directors, at the merger between the Crosby Arboretum and MSU, 1997.

ter, located in nearby Biloxi. Coastal Research and Extension already had a number of facilities in south Mississippi, including five Agricultural and Forestry Experiment Station units. Research and Extension priorities include horticulture, beef cattle production, seafood safety, natural resource economics, and coastal ecology. Dr. David Veal was head of the Coastal Research and Extension Center and directly managed the Crosby Arboretum facility. Through his leadership and belief in the value of the arboretum, he shepherded the facility through some difficult times. Dr. Patricia Knight succeeded Dr. Veal as head, and her horticultural and management expertise has benefited the arboretum immensely. The Crosby Arboretum Advisory Board retains the corporate knowledge and original vision of the facility, and assists MSU with further phases of the arboretum's development.

The mission of the Crosby Arboretum supports the directives of MSU and the Extension Service. The MSU Extension Service provides research-based information, educational programs, and technology transfer focused on issues and needs of the people of Mississippi, enabling them to make informed decisions about their economic, social, and cultural well-being.[6] Agriculture and natural resources, family and consumer education, enterprise and community resource development, and 4-H youth development are Extension's ongoing priorities, or "base programs." As at the Crosby Arboretum, Extension's overall purpose is education—education that will empower people to make intelligent decisions relating to their vocations, their families, and their environment.

Considerable effort was made in the 1990s and subsequent decades to continue building the arboretum's Master Plan infrastructure. The Savanna Exhibit needed additional trails to serve as safety fuel breaks for its annual prescribed burns. Before construction of the pathways, the firebreaks were maintained as exposed areas of soil. Over two and a half miles of trails have been constructed as walking journeys throughout the arboretum's exhibits since 1990.

After Pinecote was opened full-time to the public, there was an increased demand from visitors for interpretive signage along the pathways. However, there was little money available for the arboretum to purchase commercially produced signs. I designed a signage system for Pinecote that could be produced in-house and was inexpensive and portable. Using the pavilion posts as inspiration, staff scored and stained wooden posts to reflect the pavilion's architecture. A movable signage system allowed for temporary events, such as a wildflower coming into bloom or perhaps the discovery of a bird's nest, to be identified and described to viewers. The current interpretive signage along the arboretum's journeys offers brief descriptions of numerous natural and cultural phenomena found at the site, from descriptions of exhibit soils to insects, fungi, plants, wildlife, ecology, management practices, exhibit designs, and cultural history.[7]

New ideas were emerging of how to interpret the landscape along the trails. The goal was to expose visitors to a wide range of topics about the Piney Woods landscape and to convey its value and intrinsic worth. Reflecting on the various cultures that called the Piney Woods home, I made a new effort to develop pathway signage that would communicate how different people looked at the landscape, through their eyes and in their own words. From this exercise emerged the idea of the "dedication trail."

The first such dedication trail was developed in 1997 with assistance from Dr. John Guyton, an MSU education specialist. This particular trail features the words and observations of the naturalist William Bartram, a plant explorer who traveled through the southeastern states from 1773 to 1776. The trail offers quotes of his travels and experiences along the landscape and paints a portrait of life in unsettled times. It presents a view of the Gulf Coast as a land populated with Native American tribes, extensive forests, and a pioneering American settlement.

Similarly, three trails were dedicated to later "travelers": Ross Hutchins, an entomologist and naturalist; William Cibula, a local mycologist who lived in the area and guided many arboretum mushroom forays; and Ed Blake, the arboretum's first director and guiding spirit. Their different perspectives and personal observations of the landscape offer new ways to understand and appreciate its qualities.

Crosby Arboretum staff members Jarrett Hurlston (*left*) and Terry Johnson (*right*), managing vegetation in the Piney Woods Lake Exhibit.

Photo courtesy of Crosby Arboretum

Breaking away from traditional arboretum design formats and utilizing natural processes to create and maintain the exhibits has allowed the Crosby Arboretum to minimize staff maintenance needs. Importantly, this has allowed for a relatively low expenditure from the arboretum's annual operating budget to maintain the grounds. One full-time and one part-time employee, augmented by other arboretum staff and a cadre of volunteers, are responsible for the management and maintenance of the now 104-acre Interpretive Center and 700 acres of arboretum natural areas. Their responsibilities include maintaining trails, setting up for programs and events, leading tours, hosting programs, overseeing volunteers, conducting prescribed burns, planting trees, managing brush, building new trails and site amenities, maintaining existing site items, repairing roads and trails, managing exotic species, and a host of other duties. Allowing the ecosystem to provide the primary services of land management enables the staff to concentrate on visitor and program needs. Through the facility's association with the MSU Extension Service, volunteers from the Master Gardener, Master Naturalist, and 4-H Extension programs have contributed greatly to the arboretum. Active engagement with the Boy and Girl Scouts of America and other local service organizations has provided project opportunities for Eagle Scouts and other groups.

The arboretum director, curator, and two staff members focus their talents and energies on admissions and gift shop sales, hosting an ambitious program and tour schedule, fundraising, writing grants, acting as community liaisons, training teachers, managing the arboretum's herbarium and library collections, membership administration, coordinating and training volunteers, and a number of other activities.

HURRICANE KATRINA

On August 29, 2005, Hurricane Katrina hit the Gulf Coast shorelines of Louisiana, Mississippi, and Alabama. By the end of its rampage, Katrina would be known as the nation's costliest natural disaster and the fifth deadliest storm on record.[8] Katrina's course passed directly over the Crosby Arboretum, and the property damage and loss

Fallen pines retained in the Savanna Exhibit after Hurricane Katrina.

Photo by Ed Blake Jr., courtesy of Marilyn Blake

of timber in the area were staggering. It was estimated that 521 million trees in Mississippi alone were damaged or destroyed.[9] A few of the arboretum's natural areas bore heavy tree losses, including those at Mill Creek and Dead Tiger Savanna. Pinecote lost a few dozen trees, mostly overstory pines. Pinecote Pavilion's roof was moderately damaged by the fall of an adjacent pine, but remarkably that was the extent: the pavilion had withstood intense hurricane-force winds. The exhibits and infrastructure of Pinecote survived the devastating storm with relatively little impact, which further demonstrated their resilience. The arboretum's artesian drinking fountain flowed continuously while the area's electrical power remained disrupted for weeks, and served as one of the few non–bottled drinking water sources for the surrounding community.

The arboretum closed for four months after the storm as its staff and volunteers cleared and cleaned the trails of debris. Many of the fallen trees were left in the exhibits to decay naturally as a reminder of the tragic storm and as part of the natural cycle. Donations poured in from arboretum members to help with recovery efforts, as well as from gardens and horticultural societies across the nation. The Crosby Arboretum fared much better than many of its peer institutions devastated by the storm, such as the New Orleans Botanic Garden in City Park, which suffered heavy losses and had to be completely replanted.

The arboretum's recovery after Hurricane Katrina testifies to the wisdom of its founding concepts. By incorporating the remarkable resilience of the Gulf Coast ecosystem as its exhibit structure, the arboretum recovered quickly with minimal loss while other institutions had to rebuild at a much greater expense. The Crosby Arboretum serves as a model for the wise management of lands along the turbulent Gulf Coast ecosystem.

The Crosby Arboretum continues to build the infrastructure of its award-winning Master Plan. Fundraising drives support the construction of new pathways and new exhibits. The paths are constructed in-house by arboretum staff and volunteers and offer a relatively inexpensive way of installing infrastructure. Eleven landscape interpretive stations are proposed to be dispersed throughout Pinecote's exhibits and have yet to be fully completed. The landscape interpretive stations are intended to be gathering places located in the middle of specific habitat types. Their purpose is to distribute visitors throughout the site, and offer them a chance to rest and gather and become a part of that area's ambiance. The interpretive stations are designed to contain small structures that will display information about the nearby plant communities.

The implementation of the interpretive spaces was intended to be incremental over time. Mimicking organic growth and development, these interpretive stations begin first as a simple kiosk board with information, and then are tested to see how visitors respond to the space. This allows for needed changes to occur in the design as the interpretive stations grow into a full-fledged exhibit. Materials, forms, textures, and character are intended to evolve from their specific individual places through time. As stated in Pinecote's Master Plan, "All are conceived and placed so that each is an organic component of the system and its hierarchy."[10] This unity is a variation on a central theme first established by Fay Jones through the Pinecote Pavilion. As understanding of natural systems and new methods of technology increases, the facility can continue to utilize mechanisms to further educate the public about the arboretum's mission.

FUTURE PHASES

> Style shouldn't be the major element of design, it should instead be creating the design from the environment, from the forms. Each artist and architect will do that just like Fay Jones, but with different shapes and materials. Inspiration from the same thing is what remains constant, all you are doing is changing the interpreter.
> —Robert Poore, 2011

As the staff continues efforts to further implement the Crosby Arboretum Master Plan, Pinecote's progress will be honed and refined. The completion of the remaining site infrastructure will allow the arboretum to focus on what it does best: conduct programs and serve as a community resource. This commitment to education and community engagement is a priority. The Crosby Arboretum Foundation is conducting an active campaign to replace the arboretum's temporary facilities with permanent structures. Over the years, there have been several conceptual designs for a permanent education center to be located on the grounds. The education center's purpose is to house staff administrative offices, a library and conference room, a retail shop, and a room to host larger audiences for programs. It will also serve as a facility for community needs.

EPILOGUE

The Crosby Arboretum is also a form of development and upon its
completion has the opportunity to demonstrate a remarkable array of
alternate techniques which can be displayed, monitored, implemented, and
promoted.

—Andropogon Associates, "Outline for Developing the First-Year
Program of the Crosby Arboretum," 1983

The Crosby Arboretum is dedicated to showing and explaining to visitors how natural processes work in the Piney Woods region of the Gulf Coast. Future generations will see a much different forest, just as early visitors saw the transformation of young shrubs from an open field. When they considered its possibilities as an educational facility, Crosby's founders looked around with fresh eyes and responded in new voices. Ed Blake observed that the arboretum "pioneered ways of re-thinking and re-making our place in nature. It is an early initiative of developing a living structure, a green building, in ways that enable this world's living infrastructure, in partnership with humans, to re-make itself in sustainable ways."[1]

Thirty years after the Crosby Arboretum's conception, sustainability has become a major goal of many new architectural and landscape projects. Two organizations have become prominent leaders in the promotion of sustainable projects: Leadership in Energy and Environmental Design (LEED) and the Sustainable Sites Initiative (SITES). LEED has set the architectural standards for structures and neighborhoods to achieve minimum criteria for sustainable buildings.[2] SITES defines the categories and standards for a project's sustainable landscape development.[3] Both of these certifications help to establish important measurable qualities of sustainable planning, design, and construction. But well before the green emphasis of the landscape and architectural professions, Andropogon Associates and Fay Jones had set new parameters for ecological and sustainable design in both landscape architecture and architecture at the Crosby Arboretum. Deep-seated beliefs in a synergistic harmony between human needs and the natural world motivated these accomplishments.

The core principles established by Andropogon Associates for the Crosby Arboretum still resonate today as important criteria to establish a living, thriving sustainable landscape. Applying these key ecological concepts to our gardens and public spaces allows for the dynamic nature of life in which to shape our environments. Many management strategies used today do not encourage the conditions for biological life and the utilization of ecological process. And while these modern landscapes may appear to be clean and green, they can actually be impoverished landscapes with little ecological value. It is useful to revisit a few key principles adopted by the Crosby Arboretum to remind us of how they apply to our own landscapes:

ECOLOGICAL DESIGN
The ecological processes of the site would determine Crosby Arboretum's design and management.

The extensive studies of Pinecote's hydrology, soils, vegetation, microclimates, and other factors directed placement of all buildings and exhibits. The locations of drier soils governed where structures would occur, thus preventing costly soil excavation and replacement, and the locations of wetlands influenced where aquatic features and drainage corridors would be placed in the Master Plan. Interesting vegetative features, such as groupings of pine trees or colonies of ferns, were identified as unique features to preserve and manage. This attention to the land follows Ian McHarg's dictum to design with nature. There are plenty of projects that successfully preserve or enhance the preexisting features of a site. The American Society of Landscape Architects' annual awards program and SITES's case studies often display successful projects that showcase excellent design married with good landscape ecology.

The emerging field of urban landscape ecology is deconstructing the perceived barriers between "natural places" and urban ones by recognizing that all landscapes add or take from a functioning ecosystem. Our land management choices and strategies determine the level of an urban space assessment of its actual ecological value. The Crosby Arboretum, the Cedar River Watershed Education Center near Seattle, and the Lady Bird Johnson Wildflower Center in Austin are outstanding examples of ecologically designed landscapes. These facilities have an opportunity to teach local landowners about the design strategies and land management techniques they use, and thereby create a more informed public. Importantly, these centers discuss how healthy ecosystems can be created for a variety of land use types—whether residential, commercial, municipal, or industrial.

CHANGE
The Crosby Arboretum site will "change dramatically over time."

Faced with an abandoned pasture and scattered pine trees, the arboretum's designers knew that it would take many years to form the future forest and wetlands. The founders were also aware of the legacy they would leave to following generations. Ed Blake wrote: "In many lifetimes, a visitor to the Arboretum might stand under the heavy shade of a beech and magnolia woods where I once stood under pine trees crowded underneath by a juvenile understory of bayberry, gallberry, huckleberry, sweetbay, yaupon, gum, persimmon, oak, and jasmine."[4]

This recognition of the concept of landscape change accommodated not only the changes wrought by the maturing of the woodlands but also unplanned impacts from storms, accidental fires, droughts, floods, insect outbreaks, and climate. While these interruptions often happen with alarming regularity, we tend to think of them as anomalies. However, nature doesn't stand still, and disturbance-prone ecosystems, such as the fire-adapted Piney Woods, can more readily absorb periodic disruptions.

These ecosystems teach us that we should embrace concepts of change in our landscape plans. Many landowners have an ideal image in which they keep their landscapes managed in an ecological homeostasis. But without some built-in system of renewal, entropy sets in and the landscape goes into physical decline. Landscape architects often sustain the myth of the steady-state system by providing rendered plans of the fully mature landscape that are supposed to somehow persist through time. Using nature as a model, landscapes in the southeastern United States mostly fall into forest or grassland vegetative patterns, or some variation between. Understanding successional processes in the landscape, whether its plants are native or exotic, allows for a better grasp of why those weeds keep popping up in a sunny landscape or why certain plants won't grow under a shade tree. Some plants are better adapted to certain successional stages, and will either phase out from increasing shade or be renewed through regular disturbance. It is advantageous to know what stage of succession a landscape is in and its trajectory, and to build with the concept that change is destined to happen in and around it.

SLOW LANDSCAPES
Growth and development of the Crosby Arboretum would be slow and incremental.

The Master Plan for the Crosby Arboretum has not been completely carried out as envisioned, nor probably will it be "finished" in the near future. While it is conceivable that the infrastructure could have been completed in its first few years, the result would have been an arboretum very different from what we see today. If the earliest master plans had been followed as drawn, the buildings would have been dense and concentrated, the paths poorly integrated into their locations, the natural areas never conceived, and the work of Fay Jones never built. Instead, time and talent allowed the dream to grow and mature more fully, carefully, and deliberately.

Temporary interventions on the site allowed Crosby designers to study their effects before fully committing the arboretum's resources. Mowing the outline of the Piney Woods Lake Exhibit, which could easily be changed and manipulated, permitted Blake to make adjustments to its configuration. Only when its shape was fully absorbed and studied from various perspectives, in different seasons and light, was the excavation line determined. Similarly, before a building was constructed, "temporary" centers were installed and tested at the proposed locations. Interpretive kiosks were built where interpretive centers will be constructed, and the metal-clad Temporary Visitors Center and Restoration Center hold the ground where permanent facilities will one day exist. If a temporary center doesn't function well, it will be readily apparent. Testing the design may be difficult for projects that have urgent needs or tight deadlines, but it is always preferable to living with preventable mistakes revealed after resources have been fully allocated.

PROXIMITY MANAGEMENT

Habitat management will be greatest near the arboretum's visitor center and major visitor nodes and transition toward unmanaged near the outer edges.

First broached by Dr. Tang, this simple statement became an important management consideration. Limiting the areas cared for was crucial as there are not enough staff members or volunteers to fully manage the exhibits at a 104-acre arboretum. Prioritizing the areas for management has allowed staff to focus its abilities on programs and oversight of critical areas. Receiving most attention are trail maintenance, Savanna Exhibit management, the front visitors' parking area, the visitor center, and Pinecote Pavilion. Trails are maintained to be free of debris and to convey a clear pathway line; outside of the managed line, the exhibit's plants are allowed to be themselves and to express their nature.

Prioritizing the management of our landscapes is a difficult task. Too often, a property is mowed, raked, sprayed, and groomed—even if there is no one to see it. Overly groomed landscapes can work against their ecology. Brush piles are important for wildlife habitat and protection, leaves return important nutrients to the ground, and unmown sections of landscapes provide places for plants and animals to live.

The Crosby Arboretum, MSU Extension Service, will not be without its challenges. As Carol Franklin advised recently, Pinecote's future designers "can't violate the vision. If you get an architect that does shopping centers you are going to get a shopping center.

It's got to be a creative person like Fay Jones, an imaginative genius that springs out of the landscape like Fay Jones."[5]

The Crosby Arboretum was an experiment in ecological design, yet it also serves as a model for other landscapes that can be conceived, designed, and implemented on a more modest scale. Its founders and designers correctly assumed that by allowing natural vegetative succession to occur on a site, even if it had been previously disturbed, an outstandingly beautiful garden can result that achieves a strong sense of regional expression and serves to educate the public about its unique and important ecological qualities. Significantly, the Crosby Arboretum demonstrates that this type of garden can be accomplished with modest construction and operational budgets.

Chris Wells noted in 1984: "Unfortunately, at this stage in man's education, we know more about how to manipulate our environment than we do about the long term effects of that manipulation."[6] We must continue to measure and assess the biological capacities of built environments for a variety of spatial scales—from local parks to larger-scale greenways and transportation corridors. Biologists are now recognizing that urban and suburban landscapes play an important, if not critical, role in the sustenance of local native plant and animal systems. Daniel Botkin emphasized in 1997 that opportunities for nature within city environments need to be investigated in a fresh light and stated that, "If we are to practice biological conservation, and also create environments pleasing to people, then we need a renewed emphasis on the positive aspects of urban environments."[7] In other words, in addition to needing to expand our wilderness preserves to conserve biodiversity, our next frontier in conservation biology is the urban ecosystem.

Importantly, *people* benefit from the enhanced biological richness in their local living environments that comes via more exposure to natural systems. Regional ecology and its varied interpretations provide for a textured sense of place contrary to some designers' claims that incorporating ecology into landscape design somehow limits creative or artistic expression. But as shown through the award-winning designs of the landscape architects of Andropogon Associates, Jones and Jones, and Michael Van Valkenburgh Associates, there are rich opportunities to continue the exploration of artistic statements that are coupled with tangible, ecologically based designs.

Now, more than ever before, is the time for such designs to emerge because it is only through education and regional awareness that we will become more conscious of the roles we must play in our communities as environmental stewards. Perhaps this was best stated by British landscape architect John Brookes, who observed that "gardens are a reflection of the age in which they are created. Their style is determined by function . . . tempered by the way in which [they are] built, based on the materials at the time . . . The good ones remain because they worked."[8] The Crosby Arboretum is the product of an enlightened approach to design. Its success is due to how it was built: philosophically, environmentally, and physically; and if Brookes is right, the Crosby Arboretum will fulfill its role for a long time to come.

Awards Received by the Crosby Arboretum

AWARDS FOR PINECOTE PAVILION

1987	American Wood Council Honor Award
1987	Honor Award, Gulf States Regional Council, American Institute of Architects
1990	Honor Award, American Institute of Architects
1999	Mississippi Landmark designation, Mississippi Department of Archives and History

AWARDS FOR THE CROSBY ARBORETUM

1985	Merit Award, Mississippi Chapter of the American Society of Landscape Architects
1985	Bronze Award, Greater Jackson Advertising Club
1990	Environmental Awareness Award: Design, Development, and Management of the Landscape, Mississippi Chapter of the American Society of Landscape Architects
1991	Honor Award, Design, American Society of Landscape Architects
1991	Environmental Awareness Award, Mississippi Chapter of the American Society of Landscape Architects
1992	Governor's Award for Excellence in the Arts: Design of Public Space, Mississippi Arts Commission

1992	President's Award of Excellence, Mississippi Chapter of the American Society of Landscape Architects
1992	Merit Award, Mississippi Chapter of the American Society of Landscape Architects, Wetland Policy of the American Society of Landscape Architects
1992	Merit Award for Communications, *Native Trees* brochure, Mississippi Chapter of the American Society of Landscape Architects
1992	President's Award of Excellence, *Arboreport 3.3,* Mississippi Chapter of the American Society of Landscape Architects
1992	Outstanding Contribution Award, U.S. Fish and Wildlife Service
1993	Special Merit Award, Mississippi Wildlife Federation
1994	Conservation Award, Mississippi Wildlife Federation
1999	Medallion Award, American Society of Landscape Architects

NOTES

PREFACE

1. Polk, cited in John H. Napier III, *Lower Pearl River's Piney Woods: Its Land and People* (Jackson: University Press of Mississippi, 1985), 13.

2. Robert Brzuszek, "Establishing Spatial Patterns for the Beech-Magnolia Exhibit in the Crosby Arboretum of Picayune, Mississippi" (master's thesis, Louisiana State University, 1990).

1. THE LAND AND ITS PEOPLE

1. "Professional Awards," *Landscape Architecture Magazine,* American Society of Landscape Architects (ASLA), November 1991.

2. Roy B. Van Arsdale and Randel T. Cox, "The Mississippi's Curious Origins," *Scientific American,* January 2007, 79.

3. Grover E. Murray, "Cenozoic Deposits of Central Gulf Coastal Plain," *American Association of Petroleum Geologists* 31 (1947): 1843–48.

4. Robert Ricklis and Richard Weinstein, "Sea-Level Rise and Fluctuation along the Texas Coast: Exploring Cultural-Ecological Correlates," in *Gulf Coast Archaeology: The Southeastern United States and Mexico,* ed. Nancy M. White (Gainesville: University Press of Florida, 2005), 108–54.

5. James B. Elsner, Thomas Jagger, and Kam-Biu Liu, "Comparison of Hurricane Return Levels Using Historical and Geological Records," *Journal of Applied Meteorology and Climatology* 47 (2008): 368–74.

6. William J. Platt, "Southeastern Pine Savannas," in *Savannas, Barrens, and Rock Outcrop Communities of North America,* ed. Roger C. Anderson, James S. Fralish, and Jerry M. Baskin (Cambridge, U.K.: Cambridge University Press, 1999), 23–51.

7. "The Big Picture," Longleaf Alliance, accessed June 27, 2012, http://www.longleafalliance.org/longleaf-pine/the-big-picture.

8. John F. H. Claiborne, "A Trip through the Piney Woods," in *Publications of the Mississippi Historical Society,* ed. Franklin L. Riley (Oxford: Mississippi Historical Society, 1906), 9:514.

9. C. A. Gresham, T. M. Williams, and D. J. Lipscomb, "Hurricane Hugo Wind Damage to Southeastern U.S. Coastal Forest Tree Species," *Biotropica* 23.4 (1991): 420–26.

10. Anna King, "State and National Champion Longleaf Pine," *Mississippi Forestry Commission News,* February 2007, 1.

11. Janisse Ray, *Ecology of a Cracker Childhood* (Minneapolis: Milkweed, 1999), 164–65.

12. "Longleaf Pine Range-wide Conservation Initiative," U.S. Fish & Wildlife Service, October 2009, accessed October 18, 2012, http://www.fws.gov/southeast/SHC/pdf/LongleafPineLCC.pdf.

13. Logan Yonavjak and Nick Price, "COP-10 Provides Opportunity to Recognize Biodiversity at Home," World Resources Institute, accessed July 5, 2012, http://www.seesouthernforests.org/news/cop-10-provides-opportunity-recognize-biodiversity-home.

14. "The Longleaf Pine: Mapping the Future," Conservation

Fund, accessed June 29, 2012, http://www.conservationfund .org/strategic_conservation/long_leaf_pine_mapping.

15. Ben Raines, "No Federal Protection for Gopher Tortoises under Endangered Species Act," *Mobile Press-Register,* July 27, 2011, accessed February 5, 2013, http://blog.al.com/ live/2011/07/no_federal_protection_for_goph.html.

16. D. Craig Rudolph and Richard Conner, "Cavity Tree Selection by Red-Cockaded Woodpeckers in Relation to Tree Age," *Wilson Bulletin* 103.3 (1991): 458–67.

17. J. M. Huffman, "Historical Fire Regimes in Southeastern Pine Savannas" (Ph.D. diss., Louisiana State University, 2006).

18. Smith, quoted in Michael Williams, *Americans and Their Forests: A Historical Geography* (Cambridge, U.K.: Cambridge University Press, 1989), 44.

19. W. C. Corsan, *Two Months in the Confederate States: An Englishman's Travels through the South,* ed. Benjamin H. Trask (Baton Rouge: Louisiana State University Press, 1996), 43.

20. Cynthia Fowler and Evelyn Konopik, "The History of Fire in the Southern United States," *Human Ecology Review* 14.2 (2007): 165–76.

21. William Bartram, *The Travels of William Bartram: Naturalist Edition,* ed. Francis Harper (Athens: University of Georgia Press, 1998), 149.

22. Hazel Delcourt and Paul Delcourt, "Pre-Columbian Native American Use of Fire on Southern Appalachian Landscapes," *Conservation Biology* 11.4 (1997): 1010–14.

23. Stephen Pyne, *Fire in America: A Cultural History of Wildland and Rural Fire* (Princeton: Princeton University Press, 1982).

24. Ming-Yih Chen, Earl J. Hodgkins, and W. J. Watson, "Prescribed Burning for Improving Pine Production and Wildlife Habitat in the Hilly Coastal Plain of Alabama," Bulletin 473, Alabama Agricultural Experiment Station, Auburn University, September 1975.

25. Robson Bonnichsen and Karen L. Turnmire, "An Introduction to the Peopling of the Americas," in *Ice Age People of North America,* ed. Bonnichsen and Turnmire (Corvallis: Oregon State University Press, 1999), 1–26.

26. John H. Napier III, *Lower Pearl River's Piney Woods: Its Land and People* (Jackson: University Press of Mississippi, 1985), 21.

27. Richard Campanella, *Bienville's Dilemma: A Historical Geography of New Orleans* (Lafayette: Center for Louisiana Studies, 2008), 99.

28. Arrel Gibson, "The Indians of Mississippi," in *A History of Mississippi,* ed. Richard Audrey McLemore (Jackson: University Press of Mississippi, 1973), 1:69.

29. Napier, *Lower Pearl River's Piney Woods,* 21.

30. Alcée Fortier, "Pierre Le Moyne, Sieur d'Iberville," *The Catholic Encyclopedia,* Vol. 7 (New York: Appleton, 1910), retrieved June 27, 2012, from New Advent: http://www.newadvent.org/cathen/07614b.htm.

31. Bienville journal quoted in Napier, *Lower Pearl River's Piney Woods,* 22.

32. George L. Switzer, "Some Characteristics of the Pearl River Basin: The Drainage System," *Quarterly News Journal of the Crosby Arboretum* 3.3 (Summer 1985).

33. Napier, *Lower Pearl River's Piney Woods,* 22.

34. Francis Paul Prucha, *The Great Father: The United States Government and the American Indians* (Lincoln: University of Nebraska Press, 1984), 1:206.

35. Napier, *Lower Pearl River's Piney Woods,* 41.

36. Ibid., 48.

37. Claiborne, "A Trip through the Piney Woods," 514.

38. Napier, *Lower Pearl River's Piney Woods,* 56.

39. A. James Miegs, "Lumber in Arkansas and Mississippi," *Monthly Review, Federal Reserve Bank of St. Louis,* 37.8 (August 1955): 2.

40. Yonavjak and Price, "COP-10 Provides Opportunity."

41. Stephen Lee Timme, *Wildflowers of Mississippi* (Jackson: University Press of Mississippi, 1989), 12.

42. Greg Winter, Christine Vogt, and Jeremy Fried, "Fuel Treatments at the Wildland-Urban Interface: Common Concerns in Diverse Regions," *Journal of Forestry* 100.1 (2002): 15–21.

43. "Mississippi Forest Facts," Mississippi Forestry Association, accessed August 2, 2012, http://www.msforestry.net/pdf/ july_2010_mfa_flyer_v6.pdf.

44. David H. Ciscel, "The Economics of Urban Sprawl: Inefficiency as a Core Feature of Metropolitan Growth," *Journal of Economic Issues* 35.2 (2001): 405.

2. THE STORY

1. John H. Napier III, *Lower Pearl River's Piney Woods: Its Land and People* (Jackson: University Press of Mississippi, 1985), 115.

2. Lynn Crosby Gammill, interview by author, July 2011.

3. Ibid.

4. Catherine Gyllerstrom, "Turpentine Industry in Alabama," *Encyclopedia of Alabama,* accessed July 17, 2012, http://www.encyclopediaofalabama.org/face/Article.jsp?id=h-3137.

5. Freddie Acker, interview by author, 1990.

6. "L. O. Crosby Jr. Memorial Lectures," *Quarterly News Journal of the Crosby Arboretum* 2.1 (Winter 1984).

7. James E. Fickle, "Defense Mobilization in the Southern Pine Industry: The Experience of World War I," *Journal of Forest History* 22.4 (1978): 206.

8. "The Deadliest Atlantic Tropical Cyclones, 1492–1996," National Weather Service, accessed March 6, 2013, http://www.nhc.noaa.gov/pastdeadly.shtml.

9. Napier, *Lower Pearl River's Piney Woods,* 202.

10. Both quotes are from the Gammill interview.

11. Katherine Moak Furr, interview by author, July 2011.

12. Edward L. Blake Jr., personal notebooks, 1983, in the possession of Marilyn Blake.

13. Gammill interview.

14. Edward L. Blake Jr., interview by author, January 2009.

15. Gammill interview.

16. "Research Trips," *Quarterly News Journal of the Crosby Arboretum* 1.1 (Winter 1983).

17. Gammill interview.

18. "Research Trips."

19. Gammill interview.

20. Blake, personal notebooks, 1983.

21. *Quarterly News Journal of the Crosby Arboretum* 2.1 (Winter 1984).

22. "Research Trips."

23. "Board Member: George Switzer," *Quarterly News Journal of the Crosby Arboretum* 1.2 (Spring 1983).

24. Richard Louv, *Last Child in the Woods: Saving our Children from Nature-Deficit Disorder* (Chapel Hill: Algonquin Books, 2005).

25. "Board Member: Giles has Lifelong Interest in Plants," *Quarterly News Journal of the Crosby Arboretum* 1.1 (Winter 1983).

26. "Research Trips."

27. Gammill interview.

28. Edward L. Blake Jr., "History of Crosby Arboretum" (Crosby Arboretum internal document), 2009.

29. "Consultant: Sidney McDaniel Focuses on Education, Research," *Quarterly News Journal of the Crosby Arboretum,* 3.2 (Spring 1985).

30. U.S. Department of Agriculture, Soil Conservation Service, Soil Survey of Pearl River County Mississippi, January 23, 1983, accessed April 14, 2013, http://soildatamart.nrcs.usda.gov/manuscripts/MS109/0/pearl.pdf.

31. Natural Resource Conservation Service, Southeast Coastal Plain and Caribbean Soil Survey Region website, accessed June 13, 2012, http://www.mo15.nrcs.usda.gov/.

32. "Official Series Description—Escambia Series," U.S. Department of Agriculture, Soil Conservation Service, accessed June 13, 2012, https://soilseries.sc.egov.usda.gov/OSD_Docs/E/ESCAMBIA.html.

33. L. O. Crosby III, e-mail message to author, 2012.

34. Blake, personal notebooks, 1987.

35. Michael Pollan, *Second Nature: A Gardener's Education* (New York: Dell, 1991), 53–64.

36. "Mission," Center for Southern Culture, accessed July 6, 2012, http://southernstudies.olemiss.edu/2012/02/23/mission/.

37. Blake, personal notebooks, 2006.

38. L. O. Crosby III, "Notes from the President's Desk," *Quarterly News Journal of the Crosby Arboretum,* 2.2 (Spring 1984).

39. Gammill interview.

40. Blake, personal notebooks, 2007.

41. Sidney McDaniel, "Guide to the Natural Areas of the Crosby Arboretum," published by the Crosby Arboretum, 1987.

42. Robert Brzuszek, Robert Poore, Christopher Wells, and Jim Wiseman, "Vegetation of the Crosby Arboretum Natural Areas," *Arboreport* 3.3, published by the Crosby Arboretum, 1990.

3. THE GENESIS OF THE CROSBY ARBORETUM

1. Arlette Leroi-Gourhan, "The Flowers Found with Shanidar IV: A Neanderthal Burial in Iraq," *Science,* November 7, 1975, 562–64.

2. Maggie Keswick, *The Chinese Garden: History, Art and Architecture* (Cambridge, Mass.: Harvard University Press, 2003), 51.

3. Geoffrey Jellicoe and Susan Jellicoe, *The Landscape of Man: Shaping the Environment from Prehistory to the Present Day* (New York: Thames & Hudson, 1995), 70.

4. Norman T. Newton, *Design on the Land: The Development of Landscape Architecture* (Cambridge, Mass.: Harvard University Press, 1971), 194.

5. Robert E. Grese, ed., *The Native Landscape Reader* (Amherst: University of Massachusetts Press, 2011), 5.

6. Edith A. Roberts and Elsa Rehmann, *American Plants for American Gardens* (Athens: University of Georgia Press, 1996), xvii.

7. Stuart Udall, introduction to *A Quest for Life: An Autobiography,* by Ian L. McHarg (New York: John Wiley and Sons, 1996), xii. The books mentioned are: Rachel Carson, *Silent Spring* (Greenwich, CT: Fawcett, 1962); Aldo Leopold, *A Sand County Almanac* (New York, NY: Ballantine, 1979); Ian L. McHarg, *Design with Nature* (Garden City, N.Y.: Natural History Press, 1969).

8. W. J. Cohen, "A Critical Assessment of Ian McHarg's Human Ecological Planning Curriculum at the University of Pennsylvania" (Ph.D. dissertation, University of Michigan, 2003), 46.

9. Carol Franklin, interview by author, October 2011.

10. Edward L. Blake Jr., personal notebooks, 2007, in the possession of Marilyn Blake.

11. Lynn Gammill, "Notes," *Quarterly News Journal of the Crosby Arboretum,* 1.4 (Autumn 1983).

12. Blake, personal notebooks, 1983.

13. Ibid., 1985.

14. Ibid., 2010.

15. Ibid., 1977.

16. Gammill, "Notes."

17. Robert Poore, interview by author, 2011.

18. Buckminster Fuller, *The Buckminster Fuller Challenge,* produced by the Buckminster Fuller Institute, audio recording, accessed February 5, 2013, http://vimeo.com/1163719.

19. Franklin interview.

20. Andropogon Associates, "Outline for Developing the First-Year Program of the Crosby Arboretum" (Crosby Arboretum internal document), 1983.

21. Debra L. Forthman Quick, "An Integrative Approach to Environmental Engineering in Zoos," *Zoo Biology* 3.1 (2005): 65–77.

22. Louise S. Reade and Natalie K. Waran, "The Modern Zoo: How Do People Perceive Zoo Animals?" *Applied Animal Behaviour Science* 47 (1996): 109–18.

23. Andropogon Associates, "Outline for Developing the First-Year Program."

24. Ibid.

25. Ibid.

26. Ibid.

27. Ibid.

28. Blake, personal notebooks, 1983.

29. Ibid.

30. Ibid., 1985.

31. Lynn Crosby Gammill, interview by author, July 2011.

32. Blake, personal notebooks, 1985.

33. John O. Simonds, *Landscape Architecture: A Manual of Site Planning and Design* (New York: McGraw-Hill, 1998), 368.

34. Brian Swimme and Thomas Berry, *The Universe Story:*

From the Primordial Flaring Forth to the Ecozoic Era (San Francisco: Harper, 1994).

35. Daniel Earle, e-mail message to author, 2012.

36. Matthew Potteiger and Jamie Purinton, *Landscape Narratives: Design Practices for Telling Stories* (New York: John Wiley and Sons, 1998), 59.

37. Gammill interview.

38. Blake, personal notebooks, 2006.

39. Ibid., 2004.

40. Ibid., 2003.

41. Agnes Grinstead Anderson, *Approaching the Magic Hour: Memories of Walter Anderson* (Jackson: University Press of Mississippi, 1989), 96.

42. Patricia Pinson, "The Harmonious Art of Walter Anderson," in *The Art of Walter Anderson,* ed. Pinson (Jackson: University Press of Mississippi, 2003), 9.

43. Blake, "Profile."

44. Blake, personal notebooks, 2009.

45. Carol Franklin, e-mail message to author, 2012.

46. Blake, personal notebooks, 1985.

47. Bob Grese, e-mail message to author, 2012.

48. Franklin interview.

49. Russel Wright, *A Garden of Woodland Paths* (Garrison, N.Y.: Manitoga, 1970), 2.

50. Blake, personal notebooks, 1986.

51. Blake, "Profile."

52. Jory Johnson, with photography by Felice Frankel, *Modern Landscape Architecture: Redefining the Garden* (New York: Abbeville Press, 1991), 129.

53. Potteiger and Purinton, *Landscape Narratives,* 53.

54. Franklin interview.

55. Blake, personal notebooks, 1984.

56. Edward L. Blake Jr., "Director's Notebook: Lake to Provide Plant Diversity," in *Quarterly News Journal of the Crosby Arboretum,* 2.4 (Autumn 1984).

57. Blake, personal notebooks, 1983.

58. Ibid., 1985.

4. THE ARCHITECTURE OF FAY JONES

1. "Consultant: Fay Jones Begins Design for Visitors Center," *Quarterly News Journal of the Crosby Arboretum,* 3.1 (Winter 1985).

2. *Sacred Spaces: The Architecture of Fay Jones,* video recording, 2009, produced by Arkansas Historic Preservation Program.

3. Ibid.

4. "Consultant: Fay Jones Begins Design."

5. Lake Douglas, "The Poetics of Revealed Construction," *Progressive Architecture,* February 1987, 107.

6. "Plans Approved: Pavilion, Center Are One with Nature," *Quarterly News Journal of the Crosby Arboretum,* 3.3 (Summer 1985).

7. Maurice Jennings, interview with author, 2011.

8. Gareth Fenley, "Light and Shadow Only Decoration Park Shelter Needs," *Architectural Lighting* (March 1988): 27.

9. "Plans Approved."

10. Robert Adam Ivy Jr., *Fay Jones: The Architecture of E. Fay Jones, FAIA* (Washington, D.C.: American Institute of Architects Press, 1992), 78.

11. Ibid., 23.

12. Jennings interview.

13. "Plans Approved."

14. "Consultant: Fay Jones Begins Design."

15. "Member's Preview: New Facilities Open to Public," *Quarterly News Journal of the Crosby Arboretum,* 4.4 (Autumn 1986).

16. Paul Reyes, "Stressing the Light: The Style and Mind of the Great American Architect, E. Fay Jones," *Oxford American* (Fall 2005), 101.

17. Ivy, *Fay Jones,* 23.

18. "Architects Study Pinecote," *Quarterly News Journal of the Crosby Arboretum,* 12.1 (Winter 1994).

19. Edward L. Blake Jr., résumé for Alumni Award at Mississippi State University, 1994.

20. Mario Livio, *The Golden Ratio: The Story of Phi, the*

World's Most Astonishing Number (New York: Broadway Books, 2002), 8.

21. Fenley, "Light and Shadow Only Decoration Park Shelter Needs," 25.

22. Wright, quoted in Ivy, *Fay Jones*, 22.

23. Edward L. Blake Jr., "Crosby Arboretum Master Plan," draft narrative (Crosby Arboretum internal document), 1992.

24. Ivy, *Fay Jones*, 26.

25. Fay Jones, transcript of 1992 Gold Medal acceptance speech, University of Arkansas Special Collections, accessed April 10, 2013, http://www.uark.edu/jones/JonesAIAspeech.pdf.

26. Ivy, *Fay Jones*, 28.

27. Edward L. Blake Jr., personal notebooks, 2005.

5. DESIGN AND CONSTRUCTION OF THE PINEY WOODS LAKE

1. Edward L. Blake Jr., "Director's Notebook: Lake to Provide Plant Diversity," *Quarterly News Journal of the Crosby Arboretum,* 2.4 (Autumn 1984).

2. Carol Franklin, interview with author, October 2011.

3. Blake, "Director's Notebook."

4. Ibid.

5. Franklin interview.

6. Blake, "Director's Notebook."

7. Ibid.

8. Ibid.

9. Ibid.

10. Robert Poore, interview with author, July 2011.

11. Edward L. Blake Jr., personal notebooks, 1985, in the possession of Marilyn Blake.

12. Chris Wells, "Man-Made versus Natural: The Challenge of the Piney Woods Lake," in *Quarterly News Journal of the Crosby Arboretum,* 2.4 (Autumn 1984).

13. Lake Douglas, conversation with author, 2012.

14. Gareth Fenley, "Light and Shadow Only Decoration Park Shelter Needs," *Architectural Lighting* (March 1988): 27.

15. Lynn Crosby Gammill, interview with author, July 2011.

6. THE MAJOR EXHIBITS OF PINECOTE

1. Leslie Jones Sauer, *The Once and Future Forest: A Guide to Forest Restoration Stategies* (Washington, D.C.: Island Press, 1998), 170.

2. J. Steve Brewer and William J. Platt, "Effects of Fire Season and Herbivory on Reproductive Success in a Clonal Forb, *Pityopsis graminifolia,*" *Journal of Ecology* 82 (1994): 665–975.

3. Chris Wells, "Research and Development: Key to the Arboretum's Future," *Quarterly News Journal of the Crosby Arboretum,* 6.4 (Autumn 1988).

4. Edward L. Blake Jr., "Crosby Arboretum Master Plan," draft narrative (Crosby Arboretum internal document), 1992.

5. Carol Franklin, "Memo of AA's Current Role in the Arboretum's Planning Process" (Crosby Arboretum internal document), 1988.

6. Carol Franklin, interview with author, October 2011.

7. Franklin, "Memo of AA's Current Role."

8. Tom Dodd III, interview with author, 2012.

9. Franklin, "Memo of AA's Current Role."

10. Ibid.

11. "Mississippi's Comprehensive Wildlife Conservation Strategy," Mississippi Department of Wildlife, Fisheries and Parks, Mississippi Museum of Natural Science, accessed July 16, 2012, http://www.mdwfp.com/media/63792/cwcs.pdf.

12. Ibid.

13. Dr. Bill Wolverton, interview with author, 2011.

14. Lance Gunderson, "Resilience, Flexibility and Adaptive Management—Antidotes for Spurious Certitude?" *Conservation Ecology* 3.1 (1999), accessed April 11, 2013, http://www.ecologyandsociety.org/vol3/iss1/art7/.

7. AN ARBORETUM GROWS

1. Edward L. Blake Jr., personal notebooks, 1985, in the possession of Marilyn Blake.

2. Ibid., 1986.

3. Patricia Drackett, e-mail message to author, 2012.

4. Blake, personal notebooks, 1986.

5. "Director's Notebook," *Quarterly News Journal of the Crosby Arboretum,* 15.3 (Summer 1997).

6. "Mission," Mississippi State University Extension Service, accessed October 21, 2012, http://msucares.com/about_msucares/about_ext.html.

7. Jim Wandersee and Renee Clary, "Learning on the Trail: A Content Analysis of a University Arboretum's Exemplary Interpretative Science Signage System," *American Biology Teacher* 69.1 (2007): 16–23.

8. "Hurricane Katrina," National Oceanic and Atmospheric Administration National Climatic Data Center, accessed July 16, 2012, http://www.ncdc.noaa.gov/special-reports/katrina.html.

9. Susan Owalt et al., "Hurricane Katrina Impacts on Mississippi Forests," *Southern Journal of Applied Forestry* 32.3 (2008): 139–41.

10. "Pinecote Master Plan: A Guide for Long Range Development," research report published by the Crosby Arboretum, 1994.

EPILOGUE

1. Edward L. Blake Jr., personal notebooks, 1986, in the possession of Marilyn Blake.

2. U.S. Green Building Council, "What LEED Is," accessed July 16, 2012, http://www.usgbc.org/DisplayPage.aspx?CMSPageID=1988.

3. The Sustainable Sites Initiative, accessed July 16, 2012, http://www.sustainablesites.org/.

4. Blake, personal notebooks, 1986.

5. Carol Franklin, interview with author, October 2011.

6. Chris Wells, "Man-Made versus Natural: The Challenge of the Piney Woods Lake," *Quarterly News Journal of the Crosby Arboretum,* 2.4 (Autumn 1984).

7. Daniel B. Botkin and C. E. Beveridge, "Cities as Environments," *Urban Ecosystems* 1 (1997): 6.

8. John Brookes, *The Book of Garden Design* (New York: John Wiley and Sons, 1991), 252.

BIBLIOGRAPHY OF THE
CROSBY ARBORETUM

Books

Bennett, Paul. *The Garden Lover's Guide to the South.* New York: Princeton Architectural
    Press, 2000.
Ivy, Robert Adam, Jr. *Fay Jones: The Architecture of E. Fay Jones, FAIA.* Washington, D.C.:
    American Institute of Architects Press, 1992.
Johnson, Jory, with photography by Felice Frankel. *Modern Landscape Architecture: Redefining
    the Garden.* New York: Abbeville Press, 1991.
McHarg, Ian L. *Design with Nature.* New York: John Wiley and Sons, 1992.
Napier, John H., III. *Lower Pearl River's Piney Woods: Its Land and People.* Jackson: University
    Press of Mississippi, 1985.
Polk, Noel, ed. *Mississippi's Piney Woods: A Human Perspective.* Jackson: University Press of
    Mississippi, 1986.
Potteiger, Matthew, and Jamie Purinton. *Landscape Narratives: Design Practices for Telling
    Stories.* New York: John Wiley and Sons, 1998.
Sauer, Leslie. *The Once and Future Forest: A Guide to Forest Restoration Stategies.* Washington,
    D.C.: Island Press, 1998.
Thompson, J. William, and Kim Sorvig. *Sustainable Landscape Construction: A Guide to Green
    Building Outdoors.* Washington, D.C.: Island Press, 2007.

Magazines, Journal Articles, and Newsletters

Brzuszek, Robert. "Celebrating Water at the Crosby Arboretum." *Public Garden* (October
    1994): 13–15.

———. "Developing a Heritage Festival." *Journal of Extension* 42.6 (2004), accessed April 26, 2013, http://www.joe.org/joe/2004december/iw6.php.

Brzuszek, Robert, and James Clark. "Are They Getting It? Visitors Respond to Crosby Arboretum's Ecological Aesthetic." *Landscape Architecture Magazine* (May 2007): 78–85.

———. "Visitor Perceptions of Ecological Design at the Crosby Arboretum, Picayune, Mississippi." *Native Plants Journal* 10.2 (2009): 91–105.

Crosby Arboretum. *Quarterly News Journal.* 1983 to current. Available at http://www.crosbyarboretum.msstate.edu/pages/journal.php.

Douglas, Lake. "The Poetics of Revealed Construction." *Progressive Architecture* (February 1987): 107.

Fenley, Gareth. "Light and Shadow Only Decoration Park Shelter Needs." *Architectural Lighting* (March 1988): 25–27.

Miller, Sarah Gray. "America's Best Public Gardens." *Garden Design* (1994): 34–42.

"Professional Awards." *Landscape Architecture Magazine,* American Society of Landscape Architects (ASLA) (November 1991): 73–74.

Reyes, Paul. "Stressing the Light: The Style and Mind of the Great American Architect, E. Fay Jones." *Oxford American* (Fall 2005): 86–101.

Wandersee, James, and Renee Clary. "Learning on the Trail: A Content Analysis of a University Arboretum's Exemplary Interpretative Science Signage System." *American Biology Teacher* 69.1 (2007): 16–23.

Theses and Research Reports

Brzuszek, Robert. "Establishing Spatial Patterns for the Beech-Magnolia Exhibit in the Crosby Arboretum of Picayune, Mississippi." Master's thesis, Louisiana State University, 1990.

Brzuszek, Robert, Robert Poore, Christopher Wells, and Jim Wiseman. "Vegetation of the Crosby Arboretum Natural Areas." Published by the Crosby Arboretum, *Arboreport* 3.3, 1994.

McDaniel, Sidney. "Guide to the Natural Areas of the Crosby Arboretum." Published by the Crosby Arboretum, 1987.

"Pinecote Master Plan: A Guide for Long Range Development." Published by the Crosby Arboretum, 1994.

Schwetz, Gary. "Regional Interpretation Linking Our Natural and Cultural Identities." Master's thesis, University of Delaware, 1996.

Video Recordings and DVDs

Memorial Service for Edward L. Blake, Jr. Produced by the Crosby Arboretum. Video recording. 2011.
Natural Wonders: An Orientation to the Crosby Arboretum. Produced by the Crosby Arboretum. Jackson, Miss.: Communication Arts, 1990. Video recording.
Reflections of Strength. Produced by the Crosby Arboretum. Jackson, Miss.: Communication Arts, 2008. DVD.
Sacred Spaces: The Architecture of Fay Jones. Produced by Arkansas Historic Preservation Program. Video recording. 2009.

Broadcast Interviews

"Crosby Arboretum." Interview by Walt Grayson. *Mississippi Roads,* Mississippi ETV, 2003.
"Crosby Arboretum." *Mississippi Outdoors,* Mississippi ETV, 1997.
"Crosby Arboretum." *The New Garden Television Show.* PBS, no. 712, 1995.

Pinecote Pavilion and Piney Woods Lake

Photo by Megan Bean/Mississippi State University

INDEX

moisture patterns map, *47*
Morella cerifera (wax myrtle), 21, 72, 82, 84
Morris Arboretum, Pa., 35
mountain laurel (*Kalmia latifolia*), 30
MSU Department of Forestry, 15
MSU Department of Landscape Architecture, 15
MSU Extension, merger with Crosby Arboretum, 102–6, 114
Mt. Cuba Center for the Study of Piedmont Flora, Del., 16

National Wetland Center, La., 101
natural areas. *See* Dead Tiger Creek Hammock Natural Area; Dead Tiger Creek Savanna Natural Area; Hillside Bog Natural Area; Mill Creek Natural Area; Red Bluff Natural Area; Steep Hollow Natural Area; Talowah Natural Area
nature, prospectives of, 32–34
New Orleans Botanic Garden, La., 107
Newton, Garrett, 94
Nyssa sylvatica var. *biflora* (black gum), 84, 91, 92, 94
Nyssa sylvatica var. *biflora* (tupelo gum), 82, 91

Odenwald, Neil, 16
Olmsted, Frederick Law, 33
one-toed amphiuma (*Amphiuma pholeter*), 94
orchids. *See* giant orchid; pink orchid
organic architecture, 64
Osmanthus americanus (wild olive), 29
Owen, Hap, *17*
oxbow lakes, 29, 68

Pardue, Larry, 102
parking areas, 42, 73–74, 114
parrot's pitcher plant (*Sarracenia psittacina*), 27
Pearl River, 8–9, 23, 25–26
Pearl River County, Miss., 12, 14, 29
Pearl River Drainage Basin, 23, 82, 85, 88, 101
Peltandra sagittifolia (white arrow arum), 30
Persea palustris (swampbay), 27, 30, 81, 82
pest management strategies, 88–90
Picayune, Miss., 12–13, 25, 55–56, 95
Picoides borealis (red-cockaded woodpecker), 6
Pinecote Pavilion: architecture of E. Fay Jones, 57–63; awards, 61; concept of, 66; early rendering, *59*; Hurricane Katrina and, 107; light, use of, 62; origin of idea, 56; outgrowing influences of, 64–67, 74; photos, *58, 61*
Pineland Slope. *See* Savanna Exhibit
pine lily (*Lilium catesbaei*), 28, 79
Pine Upland Flat. *See* Savanna Exhibit
Pine Woods Depression. *See* Savanna Exhibit
Piney Woods Heritage Festival, 24, 100
Piney Woods Lake Exhibit, 56, 68–74, *69, 97, 105,* 113
Piney Woods region: benefit of fires, 5–8, *7,* 11; cultural history of, 9, 23–24; timber industry in, 1, 9–10, 14. *See also* Gulf Coast
pink coreopsis (*Coreopsis nudata*), 28
pink orchid (*Calopogon tuberosus*), 81
Pinquicula sp. (buttercup), 27
Pinus elliottii (slash pine), 6, 14, 79, 84

Pinus glabra (spruce pine), 86
Pinus palustris (longleaf pine), 5–6, *10,* 11, 21, 25–28, *29,* 29–30, 79–80, *80*
Pinus taeda (loblolly), 6, 19, 84
Pitcher Plant Bog Exhibit, 55, 76, 79–81. *See also* Savanna Exhibit
pitcher plant bogs, 5, 21, 25, 27–28. *See also* Hillside Bog Natural Area
pitcher plants (*Sarracenia* spp.), 26–27, *27,* 50, 79, 80–81
planting, 81–82, 85–87, 95–97
plant propagation area, 101
Platt, William J., 78
Polk, Noel, 23
Pollan, Michael, 23
pond cypress (*Taxodium ascendens*), 28, 45, 86
Pond Journey, 64, 67, 71, 74, 83, 84
Poore, Robert, 37, 71–72
Potteiger, Matthew, 46, 54
proximity landscape management, 114–16
Pteroglossaspis ecristata (giant orchid), 27
Purinton, Jamie, 46
Pyne, Stephen, 7

quaking bogs, 30
Quercus alba (white oak), 82
Quercus falcata (red oak), 82
Quercus virginiana (live oak), 82, 86

Rana heckscheri (river frog), 94
Rana sevosa (Mississippi gopher frog), 92
Ray, Janisse, 5
Red Bluff Natural Area, 28–29
red-cockaded woodpecker (*Picoides borealis*), 6